THE HOW-TO BOOK

THE HOW-TO BOOK

by John Malone

Facts On File Publications
New York, New York • Oxford, England

The How-To Book
Copyright 1985 by John Malone

All rights reserved. No part of this book may be
reproduced or utilized in any form or by any means,
electronic or mechanical, including photocopying,
recording or by any information storage and
retrieval systems, without permission in writing
from the Publisher.

Published by Facts On File, Inc.
460 Park Avenue South
New York, New York 10016

Library of Congress Cataloging in Publication Data

Malone, John Williams.
  The How-To Book
  1. Handbooks, vade-mecums, etc. I. Title.
AG105.M22 1984 031 83-9012
ISBN 0-87196-819-3

Printed in United States of America
10 9 8 7 6 5 4 3 2 1

ACKNOWLEDGMENTS

My thanks to Bill Adler for the idea that was developed into THE HOW-TO BOOK. Many people graciously gave of their time and expertise on numerous subjects during the writing of this book, and their contributions are noted throughout. My special appreciation, as always, to Paul Baldwin and Joyce Christmas for their many excellent suggestions, as well as for keeping me laughing and therefore semi-sane.

CONTENTS

A Maze	1
Acne Agonies	2
Advice to Friends and Relatives	3
African Violets	4
Air-conditioning Efficiency	6
Ambulance Chasers	7
Answering Machine Messages	8
Attic Treasures	9
Auction Bidding	11
Audit Anxiety	12
Autograph Collecting	14
Band-Aid Removal	15
Bargains That Aren't	16
Beer Pouring	18
Bee Stings	20
Bicycle Safety	21
Boat Balance	22
Booing	24
Bouquet Barriers	26
Burns	28
Buying on Time	29
Cable TV Confusion	30
Camera Buying	31
Canny Canning	32
Car Insurance	33
Car Rental Reasoning	34
Catering Contracts	35
Cereal Choices	36
Certified Checks	37

Chain-Letter Losers	38
Champagne Corks	39
Changing Your Name	41
Choking Fits	42
Clam Digging	43
Clothing Alterations	44
Coffee Flavor	45
Common Colds	46
Compost Piling	48
Contest Choices	49
Convulsions	50
Credit Establishment	52
Crossword Quandaries	53
Customs Cues	54
Cut-rate Fares	55
Death Announcements	56
Debt Management	57
Diamond Duplicities	58
Diet Pills	59
Defrosting Refrigerators	60
Dog Bones	61
Drug Storage	62
Ear Piercing	63
Eclipse Viewing	64
Egg Boiling	66
Eggsterol	67
Electrical Plugging	68
Elevator Breakdowns	69
Engine Repairs	70
Escalator Etiquette	71
Escaping a Hotel Fire	72

Explorers Anonymous	74
Eye Irritations	75
Fabric Storage	76
Family Trees	77
Fasting	78
Fever Reduction	79
Fighting Dogs	80
Figure Skates	82
Fireworks	83
Flambe Follies	84
Flat Tire First Aid	86
Flooded Cellars	87
Food Poisoning	88
Fresh Fish	90
Frostbite Remedies	91
Funeral Costs	92
Furniture Sanding	93
Garage Sales	95
Garlic Odor	96
Gas Leaks	97
Glass Door Warnings	98
Gossip Guidelines	99
Grass Growing	100
Guests on the Hour	101
Gumming it up	102
Guns in the Closet	103
Hang Gliding Take-offs	104
Hangover Cures	105
Heart Attack Symptoms	107
Heat Reactions	108
Hiccup-ups	110
Houseplant Watering	111
House Seats for Sale	112
Impressing the Boss	113
Insomnia	114

Jangly Jewelry and Other Audience Disturbances	115
Jigsaw Puzzlement	116
Jogging Shoes	117
Johnny *Can* Read	119
Keyhole Kids	120
Kissy Kissy	121
Knives at the Ready	122
Lamb Carving	123
Laxative Usage	125
Lead Poisoning	127
Left, Right	128
Legal Linguistics	129
Letters to the Editor	130
Lightning Strikes	132
Mail-order Madness	133
Making an Entrance	134
Martini Lore	135
Mashed Potatoes	136
Mayonnaise Mysteries	137
Mousetraps	138
Mugger's Targets	139
Mushroom Gathering	140
Nosebleeds	142
Nutrition Notions	144
Obscene Phone Calls	145
Onion Peels	146
Outdoor Wiring	147
Oven Fires	148
Overdue Bills	149
Oversexed Plants	150
Oyster Shucking	151

Package Tours	153
Paper Training	154
Parrot Talk	155
Passport Applications	156
Patent Pending	158
Performing Kids	159
Pet Primacy	160
Photographing Kids	161
Picture Hanging	162
Poison Alert	163
Poison Ivy Relief	164
Pollution at Home	166
Pot Politesse	167
Power Mowers	168
Prescription Pass-ons	169
Private Detectives	170
Putting Proficiency	171
Queasy Travelers	172
Questions for Call-Ins	173
Rare Books	174
Record Book Entries	176
Resume Reasoning	177
Rice, Really	178
Right-of-way on the Water	180
Roach Wars	181
Rose Pruning	182
Running at Your Own Speed	184
Salt on Ice	185
Sand Traps	186
Seasoning and Cleaning a Cast-Iron Skillet	187
Second Opinions	188
Seedlings	189
Shaving Tips	190
Ski Waxing	191
Skidding	192
Smoke Detector Sense	193
Spaying Overnights	194
Speed-reading	195
Sprain Treatment	196
Stopped-up Sinks	197
Suicide Prevention	198
Sunburn Solace	199
Tasteful Color Combinations	200
Tick Removal	201
Tipping Abroad	202
Toy Safety	203
Traffic Ticket Tales	204
Truth in Aging	205
Umbrella Openings	206
Union Joining	208
V.D. Awareness	210
Waiter, Waiter	212
Wart Worries	213
Who's On First?	214
Wine Storage	215
Winning the Lottery	216
Xenophobic Protocol	217
Zodiac Talk	218

A MAZE

Have you ever been inside a maze? The maze is a classic plot device in novels and movies, from Michael Innes's *Hamlet, Revenge!* to Stanley Kubrick's *The Shining*. In real life, the maze that has probably been experienced by the most people is the one at the entrance to Hampton Court, Henry VIII's palace on the outskirts of London.

When you enter a maze, you quickly discover that the turn that seemed to be right is wrong. You are confronted by hedges in all directions, and the only way out is to go back from where you came.

Life, too, often seems like a maze. We turn one way and we're wrong. We turn the other way and we are, sometimes unexpectedly, right. But we usually make as many wrong turns as right ones, and it is only through perseverance and luck that we reach the center of the maze and discover its truth, or make our way back out of a maze into the clear light of day.

Many of the wrong turns we make occur for the simple reason that we don't have enough facts. Since we can't see the whole maze from above, we simply have to struggle through it as best we can.

This book is an attempt to provide a map to certain parts of the maze in which we all find ourselves. It is not a complete map—no one knows or can hope to know the whole of the maze or the entire truth. But there are many areas in which misconceptions, myths, or lack of particular knowledge can throw up walls in front of us. If we know a little more, even a very little, we may be at less of a loss.

The topics covered in this book are wide ranging. There are facts galore, based on either intensive research or interviews with experts in particular fields. But there are also a number of entries that raise questions about what is popularly accepted as "fact." "Facts" change constantly—once upon a time everyone knew that the earth was flat. Yesterday's fact can turn into tomorrow's myth. Even more curiously, as you will discover, a myth can be rediscovered as a fact.

Because "facts" are anything but immutable, the probable right way is unlikely to give us all the answers, but avoiding the wrong way on the basis of what we do know can certainly give us an edge in dealing with our often strange but always fascinating world.

So let's get down to the nitty-gritty and begin with that nittiest of subjects, ACNE AGONIES.

ACNE AGONIES

Acne affects about 85 percent of teenagers at some point during their adolescent years. Perhaps because it is so prevalent, there are innumerable myths about the causes of acne. Allergists, dermatologists, and nutritionists associated with such distinguished institutions as the Cornell University Medical College, New York Hospital, and Johns Hopkins Hospital all debunk the cherished belief that acne is caused by chocolate, french fries, or hamburgers. That will be good news to teenagers who exist on such foods and bad news to their parents who would like them to have a healthier diet. Curiously, there is some evidence that that much touted "health food" wheat germ contains oils that may increase the severity of an outbreak of acne. Peanuts are also suspect. But there is no evidence to support the belief that acidic foods such as vinegar or pickles are the villains.

The basic cause of acne is increased growth of the sebaceous glands of the skin due to a rise in the production of male hormones that exist in both sexes. As a result, tiny ducts connecting the sebaceous glands with the skin surface become plugged with oil and dead skin cells. While heredity has to take the blame for the most severe cases, the average teenager can fight the blight by using over-the-counter soaps and lotions containing such ingredients as salicylic acid and benzoyl peroxide, which help to keep the skin dry and relatively free of oil. Exposure to the sun helps, too.

But, fundamentally, all the acne sufferer can do is wait to outgrow the condition.

ADVICE TO FRIENDS AND RELATIVES

Your friend Judy can't decide whether or not to marry her boyfriend. She wants your advice.

Your sister Suzie lets her husband boss her around like a maid. Boy, would you like to give her some advice.

Your daughter-in-law hasn't the vaguest idea how to discipline a child. You don't want to intrude, but . . .

Beware!

Throughout human history, philosophers, writers, and sages of all sorts have been skeptical, and often profoundly cynical, about the giving and/or receiving of personal advice.

Publilius Syrus, circa 42 B.C., Maxim 93 :

"Old people like to give good advice as solace for no longer being able to provide bad examples."

The Earl of Chesterfield, *Letters,* January 29, 1748: "Advice is seldom welcome and those who want it most always like it least."

George John Whyte-Melville, *Riding Recollections*, 1878: "In the choice of a horse and a wife, a man must please himself, ignoring the opinion and advice of friends."

And so it goes, down to the present time.

Advice can be a sticky transaction both from the giving and the receiving ends. Even if you didn't ask for someone's advice, the person who gave it is likely to resent you for not following it. You may be angry, too, feeling pressured to do what other people think you should do. If you do take the advice, and it doesn't work out, the fat will really be in the fire.

Asking for advice about *how* to accomplish something you have decided to do on your own is one thing; asking for advice on *what* you should do, when you are uncertain of your own feelings, is another matter entirely.

Never hesitate to ask how; be very careful about asking what. Don't hesitate to answer a how question; be careful about telling anyone what to do, even if asked.

That's my advice. (None of us is immune.)

AFRICAN VIOLETS

African violets, first discovered in the mountains of East Africa in 1892 by Baron Walter von Saint Paul (hence their botanical name *Saintpaulia*), became the windowsill rage of the 1930s, and have continued to be among the most popular of all houseplants. They have also convinced a great many people that they are cursed with a "black thumb." Successful growers love them for their brilliantly colored blooms, their compactness, and the ability to bloom year-round. The less successful complain that they develop ugly dark spots on their leaves if you look at them, get droopy when they're watered, and often rot in their pots.

African violets, being so pretty and so popular, require a little special treatment. You can't go around sprinkling cold tap water all over them as you do with your other houseplants. Cold water sends them into shock; cold water on their leaves or flowers gives them spots, especially if they're in direct sunlight; and too much water rots the roots. What African violets crave is *humidity*, not a cold bath. You can create humidity by placing them on (not buried in) a tray filled with pebbles; keep the tray moist and water the plant itself only when it has dried out considerably. They grow best in plastic pots, which don't absorb water the way clay pots do. When you do water, be careful not to get any on the plant itself, and be sure that the water is tepid to warm.

And then there's the matter of proper light and temperature. African violets like a lot of bright light but not very much direct sunlight. That means that you're probably going to have to move them around according to the season. But unless you have storm windows, don't keep them on the windowsill in the winter. They won't tolerate temperatures below 68 degrees Fahrenheit.

The best solution to these light and temperature problems, according to many experts, is to grow them under fluorescent lights, where they will happily flourish on their pebble-filled trays. There is, however, one catch: the blue varities need more light than the pink and white ones do.

If you are interested enough to take the trouble to give African violets the variable attention they require, you will undoubtedly derive a lot of pleasure from the year-round blooms and impress your "black-thumbed" friends in the process. Otherwise, the right way to deal with an African violet, whether it's given to you or you can't resist buying one at the garden center, is to take reasonable care of it, enjoy its flowers while the plant thrives, and throw it out guiltlessly when it goes into a terminal pout.

AIR CONDITIONING EFFICIENCY

It's mid-June, the temperature has been in the 90s for three days and there is no end in sight. Even in the nude, with the floor fan blowing full blast, you still can't sleep. You've got to get an air-conditioner for the bedroom. Unfortunately, there's not much flexibility in your budget, so you go to the nearest retailer and tell the clerk you want the cheapest air-conditioner you can get that will cool a twelve-foot by fourteen-foot room.

Well, the clerk starts babbling on about BTUs and EERs, and recommends a more expensive model. Why do clerks always try to get you to spend more than you want? What you want is *cheap*, and forget the mumbo jumbo.

Careful: You're making a mistake.

First, let's clear up the mumbo jumbo. A BTU is a British thermal unit, and it defines the volume of heat that an air-conditioner can remove from a room in a hour. The larger the room, the more powerful unit you're going to need, thus the higher BTU. Okay, you say, but there are two air-conditioners available with the same BTU numbers; why should you buy the more expensive one?

That's where the EER, or Energy Efficiency Ratio, comes in, and if the clerk doesn't mention it, you should. Why? Because you can save yourself a small fortune in electric bills. The higher the EER, the less electricity the unit will use. So, though you might be laying out more up front for a machine with a higher EER, you save over the long run. Most retailers will have a conversion chart that will give you the EER for a given machine. If they don't, you can figure it out by dividing the BTUs by the wattage, which is recorded on a metal plate or sticker usually located behind the removable front panel.

And by the way, don't forget to wash the filter behind the front panel at least once a year and to have your airconditioner professionally serviced every two or three years. If the unit is clogged with grime, which can happen very quickly in urban areas, its EER will go down while your electricity bills go up.

AMBULANCE CHASERS

Now that lawyers are allowed to advertise their services, the ambulance chasers have come out of the closet. Just look at the Yellow Pages. They're full of ads for legal firms that specialize in accident cases and malpractice suits. Maybe you can sue someone and get rich.

Sure, you can sue, but it may take years before you collect a cent—if you ever do. The courts are already severely overburdened, and with more people suing one another every day, the situation continues to deteriorate. There's also another hidden catch to consider. Many legal firms have a come-on in their advertisements to allay your fears about the costs of suing: "No Recovery—No Fee."

Sounds like a good deal, doesn't it?

What you have to understand is that the fee is the least of it. A "fee" may be charged as a flat sum or it may be a percentage of the eventual settlement. What the ads neglect to mention is the amount you will be charged by the legal firm for expenses. Expenses are a separate issue, and they can be astronomical. You will be charged for the lawyer's time, for court costs, legal research, and the costs involved in interviewing witnesses, just for starters.

You may have an excellent case, but before you hire a lawyer, make certain that you have a concrete idea of what those "expenses" are going to amount to.

ANSWERING MACHINE MESSAGES

More Americans buy telephone answering machines every year. And every year more Americans are hanging up the moment a recorded message comes over the telephone wires. Some people hang up when they hear a recorded message because they don't want to waste time waiting for the beep that signals it's possible to record the incoming message. Others slam the phone down in irritation at the trumpet fanfares, hit songs, or excessively cute messages they're greeted with. If you have an answering machine and are disturbed by how many blanks you're getting on the tape, you might take a closer look at your recorded greeting.

But there's a much more serious problem with the greetings people record on their answering machines. Both telephone company representatives and police department spokespersons caution people about leaving recorded greetings that invite burglary. Messages that begin, "I'm sorry I'm not at home right now . . ." are nothing but an all-clear signal to the burglar who has been casing your apartment or home and keeping track of your comings and goings. Even worse are greetings like this: "I'm on vacation in Mexico, but I'll be back on the 16th." That gives the prospective burglar a couple of weeks in which to choose the best time to break into your abode.

What should you say? Keep it short, businesslike, and indefinite. The greeting most recommended is: "I'm sorry I can't come to the phone right now . . ." or a variation on that theme. Maybe you're weeding the garden, in the shower, eating dinner, or making love. Who's to know? Some callers may find that message irritating because they think you're monitoring your calls and just don't want to speak to them. But causing a little annoyance is far better than issuing open-ended invitations to your local second-story man.

ATTIC TREASURES

"It's time to get rid of all this junk."

We've all thought that at one time or another when surveying our overflowing attics (or basements). Old trunks and suitcases stuffed with God knows what, moldering cardboard boxes, broken-down furniture and piles of ancient magazines tied together with string. Why, you wonder, did you ever keep any of this stuff?

Well, you may be glad you did.

Before you decide to get rid of "all that junk" at the dump or sell it off in a "garage sale," you should carefully examine what you are getting rid of. It could be worth a great deal more than you think.

But how do you tell?

Here are a few tips gleaned from a variety of sources. Let's talk about "antiques" first. An antique is usually defined as something that was made more than 100 years ago. Antiques can vary greatly in value, depending upon their design, maker, and rarity. Condition is also a factor, but you have to be careful in that regard. A frayed quilt dating from the 1860s, for example, may not be anything you'd put on a bed, but despite it's badly worn state, it could still be valuable. Many people assume that what makes an antique quilt valuable is the intricacy and artistry of its design. And this is true in the case of some quilts of particularly striking composition. But often the value of a quilt can lie in the rare scraps of cloth used to make it: the textiles themselves and not what was done with them are what make the quilt historically significant and therefore valuable. Indeed, in many museums, you will find certain quilts hung to display the *backing* material rather than the design. So don't necessarily assume that worn means valueless.

Second, in terms of antiques, never assume that what you consider ugly is necessarily worthless. During the 1920s and 1930s, enormous quantities of heavy and ornate Victorian furniture were junked because the pieces didn't conform with "contemporary tastes." The old and the ugly have been thrown out down through the ages, which is exactly why the surviving examples of various styles are so prized.

But the things in your attic don't have to be antiques to be valuable. Be on the lookout for what are termed "collectibles." Old movie magazines and comic books, early numbers of some science fiction magazines, baseball cards, and almost anything, from toy banks to salt cellars, with a picture of one of the Disney cartoon characters (especially Mickey Mouse) are much sought after by collectors and can bring you a tidy sum.

If you think something might be a "treasure," head immediately for your local library. There's at least one book covering every kind of collectible. Familiarize yourself with the terminology so that once you start talking to a dealer you can give the impression that you know what you have is valuable. If it is at all possible, show the items to more than one dealer; in the case of furniture or paintings, take photographs of the objects. Dealers in both antiques and collectibles expect to make at least a one-third profit. But by taking the time to compare offers for your treasures, you can make sure that you are getting your fair share.

AUCTION BIDDING

Auctions, whether in front of a country barn or at an internationally famous auction house like Christie's or Sotheby Parke Bernet in New York, can be both fun and exciting. Some people attend auctions not so much to buy as for the pure drama of the situation—especially at a fine art auction where the bids on a single painting or piece of jewelry can escalate by tens of thousands of dollars in seconds. If you do go to an auction in order to buy, however, you need to know what you are doing. Many inexperienced people bid more than they can afford or get stuck with something they really didn't want to buy or discover after the fact that the piece they have bought is not in good condition.

Art dealer Peter Sherwin, of the Hanover Square Gallery in New York, suggests several points of caution for the beginning bidder. First, never bid on anything that you haven't been able to inspect beforehand to ascertain its condition. Major auction houses always display the items to be auctioned for a stated period of time before the auction actually takes place. At a country auction, arrive early enough so that you can wander around checking out possible items you might like to bid on before the auction gets underway.

Read the "terms of sale" of the auction house carefully. What forms of payment do they accept? Do they guarantee authenticity? When it comes to the actual bidding, raise your hand high. Be deliberate in your motions, but do *not* move your hands if you aren't sure you want to bid further. It does actually happen that people scratch a cheek at the wrong moment and discover they've made a bid. Make certain that you are bidding against someone else, and that the auctioneer isn't taking imaginary bids from the chandeliers in order to drive up the price artificially.

Many people feel safer and less intimidated at small-scale country auctions, but Mr. Sherwin suggests you are much less likely to get taken at a big city auction house with a long-standing reputation to maintain. The country auctioneer can spot a tourist at fifty yards and may be an expert at passing off reproductions as antiques, or driving up the bidding with a variety of tricks. There are, of course, honest country auctioneers, but if you're a stranger in the area, be wary of that kindly old "down-home" character who keeps suggesting that this or that item is "going for a song." It may well be that it really ought to be going for a single bar of music.

AUDIT ANXIETY

You are sitting across from an Internal Revenue Service officer who is going over your tax forms and the supporting evidence you have been asked to bring in. You are, at best, very nervous. The IRS examiner has asked a number of questions. Then, suddenly, there is silence, as he or she examines your receipts in connection with deductions for business lunches. The silence makes you uncomfortable. What can you say that will convince the examiner that you are an honest taxpayer and a nice person? You open your mouth to speak.

Shut it again immediately.

General accountants, tax specialists, and even former IRS employees who have "gone public" all agree. Never say anything during an audit except in answer to a specific question. Whether or not you are a nice person is of no interest to the IRS officer. More important, in the process of trying to be pleasant and cooperative, you may well volunteer information that could cost you money. Of course, when you are asked a specific question, you should answer calmly and politely. But don't run on. Not only may you inadvertently stick both feet in your mouth, but your babble will also slow down the interview. Remember that the representative you are dealing with wants to conclude matters as quickly as you do. He or she has additional cases to handle.

On the other side of the coin, don't get angry. Some people react to the stress of an audit by complaining about how high taxes are or railing against how tax dollars are spent. The officer you are talking to didn't make the laws but is simply carrying them out. If you want to complain, write your congressman or senator. Don't, even as a joke, point out that you read the other day how the Pentagon spent 100 dollars for a boot that you could buy for nine cents at the local hardware store. Even if the IRS officer personally agrees with you that such waste is shameful, he or she doesn't want to hear about it.

Finally, people who have had dealings with the IRS often offer one piece of free advice that should be totally ignored. "Listen," they'll tell you, "all they want is paper. Put everything in a suitcase and dump it on their desks and let them try to figure it out." That's a myth—although a very popular one. Throwing pounds of paper at the IRS is really, of course, a rather obvious way of expressing your fear and anger. And the response is likely to be a determination to assess you for enough tax dollars to make the time and effort of going through that mess worthwhile. That is not official IRS policy, but it does happen.

If you are called in for an audit, you will be told what papers, evidence, receipts, etc. to bring. Find them, review them, and take those, and only those, papers with you.

There is nothing to prevent you from sending your tax accountant in your stead or taking him or her with you. Even if you have done your own taxes, you can legally hire someone to represent you at any stage. But that, too, will cost you money. Many people are perfectly capable of getting through a tax audit on their own, with minimal or even no additional assessment, provided they don't volunteer information, don't get angry, bring only the papers required, and above all simply stay calm.

AUTOGRAPH COLLECTING

The more zealous sort of autograph collector is sometimes referred to as an autograph "hound." An autograph hound may, like a hunting dog, have an uncanny ability to sniff out a celebrity, but more often what he or she does is "hound" film, television, and music stars gracelessly and often at entirely inappropriate moments. There are a few stars whose egos are such that they will happily sign an autograph any time and any place, but they are exceptions. Many of them cherish their privacy, and some have been known to be extremely rude (even physically abusive in a few celebrated cases) when beset by an autograph hound.

Yet it is possible to acquire even the most celestial stars' autographs if you take the right approach. Farnham Scott, himself an actor, who starred in the movie *Fat Angels* and who has been featured in other films and in television miniseries, has been collecting autographs since he was a teenager. He suggests that the right way to go about getting a celebrity's autograph is to make it as easy as possible for the star to comply. His preferred technique is to purchase a publicity photograph himself (most large cities have several shops specializing in such material) and send it on to the star with a brief note, requesting that the photograph be signed. Do not, he advises, tell your life story or go on for paragraphs about every movie, television appearance, or concert in which the star ever appeared. They know already.

Enclose a self-addressed, stamped return envelope. By sending your own photograph of the star, you help ensure a reply—after all, it is your property. And by taking the burden off the celebrity, in terms of both time and money, you increase your chances of getting back your self-addressed envelope with that coveted autograph of, say, Elizabeth Taylor—Mr. Scott has two of hers.

BAND-AID REMOVAL

The old "quick pull" method of removing a Band-Aid or dressing tape may only "hurt for a minute," but it can certainly be painful, especially if the tape has been applied to a hairy part of the body.

As everyone knows, Band-Aids have a tendency to come off by themselves during a shower or bath, but it may be that the wound should not be subjected to water. In that case, you can easily remove the bandage by holding a hair dryer close to the tape for a few seconds. The heat will partially melt the adhesive, making it possible to pull it off with far less pain.

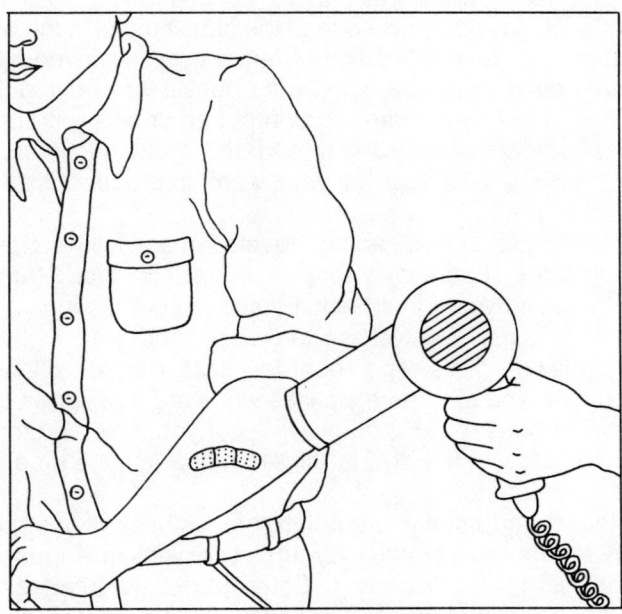

BARGAINS THAT AREN'T

Bargains Galore! Super Savings! Mammoth Markdowns! Tempted? Of course you are. Everybody likes a bargain.

But you'd better be careful. Despite the long-standing guidelines of the Federal Trade Commission concerning retail advertising, and the efforts of better business bureaus and consumer affairs departments across the country, misleading or deceptive ads still hook people into buying bargains that aren't. But you can protect yourself. There are a number of clues that you should look out for and then be doubly wary.

First, ask yourself if you can trust the ad or store poster. For example, there is the "Going Out Of Business," or "Lost Our Lease Sale." There are, of course, legitimate stores that do go out of business or lose their leases. But such sales are also one of the oldest tricks in the business. Several stores on New York's Fifth Avenue that sold everything from rugs to cameras spent years going out of business until much higher fines and possible criminal prosecution put an end to such practices. While most resident New Yorkers avoided them, the stores did a booming business with tourists who were impressed by the Fifth Avenue address.

Another example of misleading advertisement is the sign in the window that states: "Entire Inventory Reduced." "Reduced from what?" is the first question you should ask if you see such a sign.

Of course you can always ask the clerk. And you might get the reassuring answer, "This tape recorder is 25 percent off our usual price." And sure enough, there's a little white tag that shows the price marked down from $100 to $75. However, if you took the time to look further, you'd discover that $75 is still $15 more than the tape recorder would cost in most stores.

Most retailers, fortunately, are not in the business of trying to cheat you. But even reputable stores may advertise sales in language that is vague, confusing, or misleading. Some consumer magazines and books go into considerable detail trying to explain what terms like "list price," "manufacturer's suggested price," "regularly," "originally," and "usually," actually mean in various sales contexts. But the bottom line is quite simple. The more specific an ad is about what you would have paid last week, and what your savings will be if you buy this week, the clearer your understanding becomes about how much you actually are saving. Keep an eye out for the *specific* ads and tread warily if an ad is vague.

Beyond that, as every consumer advocate and agency constantly repeats, *comparison shop*. This may take time, but it is the only way to be certain that you are getting bargains that are instead of bargains that aren't.

BEER POURING

Much of a writer's research can be done sitting in a chair at a desk with time-honored tools—books, periodicals, typewriter, and a telephone. But sometimes a field trip or two is required. The sources for this particular entry were contacted at sleazy corner bars, raucous backyard barbecues, and tailgate parties.

The issue here is the foam a beer forms at the top of the glass. We need to start with a major distinction. Draft beer, from the bar spigot or the backyard keg, had better have foam on top. In fact, many guzzlers believe that about 20 percent of the glass should be foam. If you don't get foam, it means the beer has lost some of its freshness, which is what draft beer is all about (aside from being cheaper).

For bottled beer there are two camps: Those who advocate big heads and those who frown on any head at all. The big-head camp holds that beer must be poured straight down into the center of the glass so that it foams up into a big head. The foaming, they say, alloos the flavor to unfold. The no-head camp insists that you hold your beer glass, mug, or stein tilted in your hand and carefully and slowly pour the

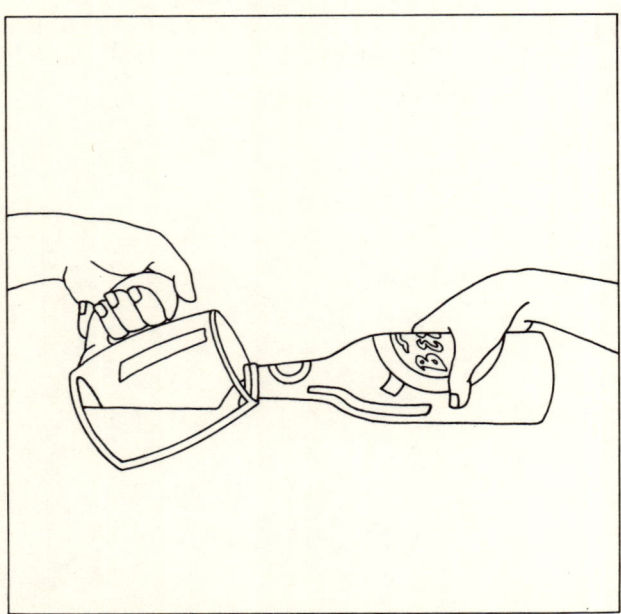

beer down the side. The beer will rise with no head at all. If you want a small head, fill the glass most of the way while it's tilted, and then set the glass straight and pour the last ounce or so down into the center.

BEE STINGS

A lot of people panic when a bee flies into a room or car or starts buzzing around in the garden. They scream and flap their arms or get up and run away. All these activities are invitations to be stung. Many other people, however, don't take the dangers of bee, hornet, and wasp stings seriously enough.

The venom of a single sting can cause an acute allergic reaction. A sting can cause almost immediate breathing problems, surging blood pressure, blackouts, and hives that may last for days. Many doctors believe that a surprising number of deaths attributed to heart attacks and strokes are really brought on by an extreme reaction (called anaphylactic shock) to the toxicity of bee venom.

How can you tell whether you might be a potential victim of that kind of severe allergic response? The trouble is that you can't. Studies by the National Institutes of Health have shown that everybody is at risk. The majority of people can be stung numerous times, with no problem aside from the immediate pain of the sting. Others, for reasons that puzzle immunologists and allergy specialists, can suddenly become allergic although they never had been before. On the other hand, some individuals may develop an immunity after several frightening episodes of allergic reactions.

What can you do to protect yourself?

First, if you or your children have even the beginning signs of an allergic reaction—hives, any kind of breathing problem following a sting, or unusual swelling around the sting—consult your doctor. An immunization treatment using bee venom may be recommended. For those who know they have venom allergies, emergency kits are available, in most states by prescription only. They contain a disposable hypodermic needle for the injection of epinephrine (adrenalin), as well as a supply of antihistamines. If someone has an allergic reaction unexpectedly, and no kit is at hand, give the person an antihistamine (even an over-the-counter asthma or hay-fever compound will help) and get him or her to a hospital.

To protect yourself from bee stings, avoid bright clothing, don't wear perfume, and don't eat sweet foods outdoors. Above all, don't panic when a bee approaches. The less movement you make, the less likely you are to be stung.

BICYCLE SAFETY

The use of bicycles has increased enormously in urban areas in recent years. Many people claim that riding a bicycle to work gets them there faster than driving a car or using public transportation. It's also good exercise. There may, however, be some health risk involved. Environmental studies in several cities have shown that bicycle riders in urban areas, like city joggers, inhale increased levels of carbon monoxide because of the heightened cardiopulmonary rate brought on by exercise.

The real problem, though, is safety. Bicycle accidents have greatly increased, often out of proportion to the number of riders. There are two categories of bicycle accidents, those in which the rider is hit by an automobile and those in which the rider knocks over a pedestrian. Police and traffic safety departments say that problems are due to the fact that so many bicycle riders invent their own rules of the road. Some zip in and out between automobiles with the crazy abandon of motorcyclists on highways. Others continually try to beat the red light at intersections—since the bike is less than half the length of the average car, they think they can just dash on through. Still others ride against the flow of traffic or go the wrong way down one-way streets.

Police spokespersons say there is only one right and safe way to ride a bicycle on city streets, and that is to follow all the traffic rules that apply to automobiles. In addition, the bicycle rider should stick to the far right lane. You may not get there as fast but you're much more likely to arrive in one piece by following the rules.

BOAT BALANCE

We've seen it a hundred times in movies. Somebody tries to get into a canoe, rowboat, small motorboat, or sailboat, and teeter-teeter-whoosh, it's into the water with them. Usually such scenes appear in romantic or slapstick comedies, and, like the classic banana-peel stunt, they're always good for a laugh. But sometimes such scenes are used seriously: think of Shelley Winters in George Stevens's classic *A Place in The Sun*, falling into the middle of Loon Lake and drowning when she suddenly tries to stand up and lunge toward Montgomery Clift.

When a boat capsizes out on the water, it is perfectly possible to be struck on the head as it overturns, or to be trapped beneath it. Even at dockside, you may fall toward the dock rather than the water, and serious injuries can occur.

But getting into or out of a small boat safely is really very simple. All you have to do is keep in mind the center of gravity, both yours and the boat's. Because the boat is floating, it will change its center of gravity as you change yours. So keep yours *low*. That means SQUAT. Hold

onto the side of the boat or canoe with one hand, put one foot into the boat as close to its center as possible, and then, still squatting, put the other foot into the craft. And sit down immediately.

You *can* stand up in a small boat once you get used to the right balance; and in a sailboat, someone has to stand up in order to get sails attached to the runners on the mast. But this shouldn't be your task unless you have some experience. If you're not used to boats, hunker down, regardless of whether you are sitting still or moving to another position.

BOOING

The million-dollar-a-year outfielder, hitless in his last six at-bats, strikes out with the bases loaded in the eighth inning and is instantly rewarded with a "Bronx cheer" by 30,000 "fans"; the quarterback is intercepted for the third time in the game and the "boo-birds," as some sports reporters call them, start giving it to him from the stands.

The soprano singing *Tosca* is off pitch throughout her famous aria, "Vissi D'Arte," and massacres her final high notes. The applause is muted, but a gentleman in the grand tier feels a more pointed response is required and loudly boos the tremulous prima donna. The people around him turn to glare or actually tell him to shut up.

If you *don't* boo in the ball park, you are likely to be regarded by the beer-swilling enthusiasts around you as something less than a real fan, or perhaps even a secret supporter of the other team. In the opera house, if you do boo you are likely to be treated as though you had slapped another man's wife.

Why is it perfectly all right to boo at a sporting event and so dreadfully wrong to do so at the opera, the ballet, or a concert? Or is it? Some sports reporters feel that, in fact, booing has gotten out of hand in the sports world and that many fans are using the occasion to vent personal angers and disappointments.

On the other hand, there are cultural observers who suggest that American audiences are far too docile at the opera or ballet. They point out that in Italy singers are routinely booed, although it may be that a rival singer has actually paid the booers to denigrate the competition, just as they pay a "claque" to *applaud* vociferously when they are singing, regardless of the quality of their performance. If you don't think this is a serious question, it should be noted that when a substitute tenor was recently booed at New York City's Metropolitan Opera, several small fights broke out in the balcony.

In deciding whether to boo or not to boo, there are several things to keep in mind. Sporting events are by their very nature aggressive contests, while the opera and the ballet are supposed to appeal to our "higher nature." Sports fans should remember, however, that by booing a player every time he makes a mistake, you may be undermining his confidence even further and making it more difficult for him to perform as you (and he) would like. A little understanding of the pressures involved would seem in order. The same goes for the singer or dancer who messes up. Sometimes, at the ballet or opera, if you want to express your displeasure most forcibly, absolute silence can be the most effective—and devastating—comment of all.

BOUQUET BARRIERS

The dining room table is resplendent with shining silver, elegant china, and glittering glassware. In the center of the table is a gorgeous tall bouquet of seasonal flowers. While that bouquet looks beautiful, it may also be all wrong. According to experts on etiquette, if the bouquet rises in height above the midchest of the shortest person you've invited to dinner, it is too tall. A bouquet that comes up to chin level will inhibit conversation between people seated on opposite sides of the table. And if the bouquet is tall enough actually to block one's view of the person opposite, it is a guarantee that dinner conversation will falter.

And yet people do it all the time. Even the dining tables of professional designers, as pictured in the pages of ritzy magazines, are often marred by overweening bouquets. The etiquette experts and the designers are often at odds on this issue. The designer may want a spectacular "look," while the etiquette expert insists that decoration should enhance, not impede, the pleasures of conversing at a social occasion.

The right way is to keep a central bouquet low enough and discreet

enough so that people don't feel that it's a barrier to human communication. Gladiolas are beautiful, but they never were intended to serve as walls between people. Put that high bouquet on the sideboard or a corner table, and let your guests dazzle one another at the table with their wit.

BURNS

If you burn yourself—be it with hot grease, boiling water, or by picking up a pot without using a pot holder—do not under any circumstances smear butter on your burn or use any other old-fashioned remedy. Those methods will only make the injury worse. There is only one right thing to do: apply cold water—either running water or a cold compress. If the burn is serious enough to have broken the skin, see a doctor.

BUYING ON TIME

Deferred payment plans can be regarded as one of the mainstays of American consumer buying, but they can also be viewed as a major contributor to the overload of cases in the bankruptcy courts. Before you buy anything—from stereo equipment to a bedroom set to a car—on time, think about:

1. How much the item is actually going to cost when you add the interest payments to the initial price; and
2. How much optional spending power you have: i.e., can you really afford the additional payments?

Many people fudge the issue on both counts.

You should find out not only the annual percentage rate but what the total cost is going to be in *dollars*. Is that $7,000 car actually going to end up costing you over $8,000? Think about what else you might want or need that extra $1,000 for. Maybe you should lower your sights.

Knowing the real dollar amount will then make it easier for you to calculate whether or not you really have enough optional spending money to afford the additional payments. To arrive at that figure, total up all your monthly expenses (with the exception of loan or credit payments)—rent or mortgage payments, utilities, food, transportation and other basics—and subtract the amount from your monthly income. Now from that result subtract the loan or credit payments you are already committed to. Doing this as a separate step will make clear how much you are already paying out in nonmortgage interest. What's left is your optional spending income.

Take a hard look at that amount. Recognize that it has to pay for things that are indeed optional but may be very important to you, from clothes to entertainment. And don't forget your vices. Do you smoke two packs of cigarettes a day or have several drinks every evening?

How many dollars out of those optional funds can you really spare to buy something else on time?

CABLE TV CONFUSION

Even insiders have a hard time figuring out the cable television industry. New cable services appear and disappear with alarming frequency. Millions of dollars are invested, millions are made, and millions are lost. Companies merge and dissolve with an Alice in Wonderland/mysteriousness and rapidity that leaves Wall Street investment analysts and creative entrepreneurs reeling. Just about the only certainty is that the shake-ups and shake-outs in the industry are likely to continue for at least another decade, by which time new technology, especially in the area of communication *through* your television set with the outside world, might well turn everything upside down all over again.

In the face of all this confusion, the wrong thing to do is to act on impulse. Don't sign up with a cable service just because it happens to be showing two movies you want to see next week. Not only *TV Guide* but also many local newspapers now carry extensive cable listings. Go over them with family members over a period of several weeks, keeping a list of programs that are of particular interest. Which service comes out ahead in terms of your overall entertainment requirements?

Of course, if expense is no object you can always subscribe to several services. But, as many psychologists emphasize, television has its undesirable side-effects, and you might consider these before going cable crazy. If you have children, how much and what kind of television do you want them to be watching? Are there arguments in your household over what program to watch even with only a few commercial channels available to you? Think about how those arguments are likely to escalate with an even greater variety. Cable television is unquestionably a wave of the future—just take care not to drown in it.

CAMERA BUYING

There is a bewildering variety of types and brands of camera on the market today, and when you add in the number of specialized lenses, filters, and flash units available, the possible combinations can make camera buying daunting in the extreme.

Before you buy a new camera, consider carefully what you want to use it for. Perhaps you merely want it for family snapshots. An "instant" camera—one that develops photos in seconds before your eyes—may be what you need. But the film for such cameras is expensive, and if you take a lot of family pictures and like to send offfcopies to relatives and friends, an automatic 35-millimeter camera may be a better bet. There are models available that take care of the focusing and the aperture opening automatically in response to available light. You can snap away without worry, get your film developed overnight at one of the numerous chains specializing in 24-hour service, and have a negative available for easy reproduction of your favorite pictures.

Or you may want to take "artistic" pictures, whether of flowers, sunsets, or landscapes. In that case you ought to be thinking about a camera that gives *you* more control over the depth of field and the lighting of the subject. Depending upon your level of expertise, you may want an automatic camera with "override" features that make it possible for you to take charge, or a semiautomatic single-lens reflex (SLR) that draws on your attention and creativity in determining the settings.

The important thing is to know what you want to do with your camera before you go to the store. Explain your needs to the clerk, and he or she will immediately be able to narrow the choices to a sensible few.

CANNY CANNING

Home canning, the putting up of fresh fruits and vegetables or the making of jams, jellies, and pickles, once practiced in all small towns and rural areas, went into a decline following World War II. The improvement of commercially frozen foods, the increasing variety of canned goods on store shelves, and the increasing number of women in the work force, all contributed to that decline. But in recent years, home canning of foods has enjoyed a resurgence, partially as a way of practicing economy, partially as a recreational outlet that may be seen as a kind of defense against the harried complexities of contemporary life, but perhaps most of all as a reaction to growing public awareness of the chemical preservatives used in commercial products.

Home canning (it should really be called home jarring, since glass containers are almost universally used these days) is great fun, and the results can be absolutely delicious. But a few words of warning are in order.

Don't follow the canning directions in the old cookbooks that belonged to your mother or grandmother. The two methods most often described in old cookbooks are dangerous. One is steam canning, which involves placing jars of food on a rack in a covered kettle and simply steaming them over a small amount of boiling water. Since the interior temperature of fresh vegetables must reach at least 240 degrees, and that of acid foods such as fruits and tomatoes (which, technically, are a fruit and not a vegetable) must reach 212 degrees, the steam-canning method may not generate sufficient heat and is unsafe. For the same reasons, never use the oven-canning technique recommended by many old cookbooks.

What method should you use? For putting up vegetables you will need to purchase a steam-pressure cooker. Steam-pressure canning is regarded as the *only* safe technique for processing vegetables, although the boiling water bath technique, in which the jars of food are fully submerged in boiling water, is safe for fruits.

The general cookbook that covers the subject most thoroughly is *The Fannie Farmer Cookbook*, Twelfth Edition (1979), published by Knopf. The Department of Agriculture has an excellent booklet available: Write to U.S. Department of Agriculture, Food and Nutrition Service, 3101 Park Center Drive, Alexandria, VA 23203.

CAR INSURANCE

You've received a substantial raise, you need a new car, and you've decided to move up to a luxury model or buy that sports car you've always wanted. But before you do, you should check out what that prestigious car is going to do to your insurance rates. Most people assume that the primary factor determining their insurance rates is their driving record—no accidents and no moving violations and your rate will be much lower, right? Not necessarily. Your safety record counts for a lot, but even if it's perfect, your insurance rate can rise dramatically according to the kind of car you own.

One reason is that a luxury car or a sports model with lots of extras costs significantly more to repair. But the main problem is car thieves. It's not that they have such good taste, but rather that they can get a lot more money for certain cars than for others. The parts for, say, a Mercedes or a Lincoln Continental, even if the car is stripped down, are worth hundreds of dollars more than those of an ordinary sedan. Insurance companies keep very close tabs on the makes of car that are enjoying a particular vogue with car thieves. They're well aware that a new model that's selling like hotcakes is also going to be stolen in increased numbers, even if it's not ordinarily classed as a luxury car. For example, since Corvettes were the most stolen car in America in 1982, insurance companies are going to hike up the rates for future buyers of this car accordingly.

So, before you buy a new car, check with your insurance company about how the model you want will affect your rates, and figure the amount into your budget.

CAR RENTAL REASONING

Riddle: When do four days amount to more than a week?

Well, suppose you want to rent a car to take a long weekend trip to the beach or the mountains. You want to pick up the car Friday noon and return it Tuesday noon. The rental company has a three-day-weekend special but you need the car for an extra day, and so you aren't eligible. You reserve a car for the full four days at the daily rate. You could be making a mistake.

It might easily be cheaper to rent the car for a week. Just as the cost of a box of laundry detergent goes down in cost per ounce as the size of the box gets bigger, so the rental rate for cars usually goes down as the length of time you keep the car increases. That's because every time a car is returned it has to be serviced, and there are also bookkeeping costs to consider. When a car is out longer, overhead is cut, and some of the savings are passed on to customers. You will, however, have to keep the car for the full week.

There are also such factors as free mileage, or the lack of it, or limitations upon it, to be considered. But it is worth sitting down and figuring out the comparative costs involved. Sometimes more is actually less.

Remember, too, that the rental car companies are as competitive as the airlines, and that there are many special deals of various sorts offered by different companies at different times of the year. Find out what's available. Shop around.

CATERING CONTRACTS

You are planning a New Year's Eve buffet, a special birthday or anniversary party, a Bar Mitzvah celebration or, God help you, your daughter's wedding reception. Whether you regard yourself as an indifferent cook, want to be able to mingle with your guests instead of sweating over the stove, or are on the verge of a nervous collapse, there seems to be only one answer: a caterer.

Jeanne Jones, author of numerous diet cookbooks, the novel *Ambition's Woman* (Evans, 1982), centered on the catering world, and a renowned California partygiver in her own right, suggests that there are several areas in which people go wrong in hiring a caterer.

First, those who are not used to dealing with a caterer may be too timid to ask for what they really want. It's true that most caterers specialize in certain types of culinary presentations, but a good caterer will help you to put a personal stamp on your party. Find out what the full range of possibilities is, and plan the menu in terms of the impression *you* want to make on your guests. Don't meekly accept the caterer's suggestions or allow yourself to be dictated to. Assert your own taste.

Second, don't hesitate to insist that the caterer pay a visit to your home, in order to ensure that the party is planned around your decor, including the color scheme of your dining room and living room and the design of your china and glassware. A good caterer will be happy to visit you, since that will make his or her planning easier as well. With first-hand knowledge of the layout of your kitchen and the equipment it contains, for example, the caterer can make his or her own job easier.

Third, make sure you understand all the ramifications of the catering contract you sign. Most caterers require a deposit, which can be as low as 15 percent, but may be much higher for a large affair. What happens if you have to cancel your party? (Illness or a quarreling bride and groom are facts of life, after all.) With sufficient notice, most caterers will return a deposit or a portion of it. But be sure to discuss the matter before signing.

Fourth, never try to change the size or scope of your party at the last minute. The logistics of catering even a small dinner party are complex, so once you decide upon the number of guests you are inviting, have the courtesy to stick with that number.

CEREAL CHOICES

The wrong way to choose a cereal for your children (or for yourself) is to pay any attention whatsoever to advertisements. It's not that they lie, but they are extremely *selective* in the selling point they focus on. One cereal may be pitched to kids; it's a "fun" cereal, perhaps even named after a popular movie, video game, or cartoon character. Another cereal will be advertised in terms of its vitamin content, while still another takes the "health" route—whole grains and no additives or preservatives. The important factor, however, is not the cereal's *image* but its *content*. To discover what the cereal actually contains, ignore the ads and read the label on the side of the box that lists ingredients and such nutritional information as the number of calories in a given portion (usually one ounce), the amount of protein and carbohydrates, and—in some cases—the vitamin content. If you take a few minutes in the supermarket to read the labels, you may be surprised to discover that the great majority of cereals have the same calorie count: 110. With the addition of a half cup of milk, the calorie count goes to 190. Of course, if you eat two ounces of the cereal with the same amount of milk, the calorie count leaps to 300.

The protein listings are interesting, too. The majority of the cereals provide 2 percent of the U.S. Recommended Daily Allowance of protein. Adding the milk brings the percentage up to 10. Thus you consume 110 calories of cereal to get only 2 percent of the USRDA of protein; while the half cup of milk will give you five times as much protein for 30 fewer calories. With another couple of tablespoons of milk you could get all the protein and forget about the cereal altogether.

There are some "natural" or "whole grain" cereals that offer more protein (about twice as much, i.e., 4 percent of the USRDA) and fewer calories (80 to 90), and they do help to get more fiber into your diet. But you may not be able to get your kids to eat them without adding sugar. There are also a few cereals of the "puffed" variety that contain only 50 calories an ounce. These cereals, however, contain virtually no protein.

Then, too, there is the question of vitamins. Some cereal products are advertised as being "enriched" or "fortified" with vitamins and minerals, which means the vitamins have been added by the manufacturer. A person who eats well-balanced meals has no need of the extra vitamins that are loaded into cereal products.

Last but far from least, you will want to take note of the sugar and salt content of various brands of cereals, as well as the chemical additives.

The choice is yours. But at least find out what you are choosing.

CERTIFIED CHECKS

The moving company insists that you pay them with a certified check. You're making the down payment on a house or a new car: a certified check, please. The reason you're asked for a certified check is that it's just as good as cash and it can't bounce.

It's true that a certified check won't bounce, but only in certain circumstances *dictated by the bank* is it just as good as cash. In most cases the certified check will be cashed immediately by the original *issuing* bank. If you deposit it at a branch office, it should be credited the next day. But if you try to cash or deposit a certified check at another bank or in another state, it will be treated like an ordinary check. Either the bank will refuse to handle the check at all (because "bank policy" forbids cashing checks of those who don't have accounts); or the bank will insist on the usual number of days to process an out-of-state check. "Bank policy" has clearly grown up to serve the interests of the bank. Although they could cash the certified check immediately and collect the money through computer transfer, within 24 hours, bank policy allows them to sit on and use the money for up to a week, depending on state law.

If you want to get emergency money to someone quickly and reliably, wire it, either to a specific account at a specific bank, or via Western Union. Certified checks won't bounce but there's no way they're as good as cash.

CHAIN-LETTER LOSERS

There are two kinds of chain letters: those that promise to make you rich, and those that threaten death if you don't send out 20 copies within the next 48 hours. The money kind of chain letter was started by someone who probably has made a lot out of the deal. Such people are con artists; what they're doing is against federal law, and they are counting on your greed. The second kind of chain letter, which might be termed the "have faith" letter, was started by a kook, is almost always illiterate, and uses fear and superstition to egg you on.

Out of hope and greed, a lot of us actually choose to believe that somebody else received three thousand dollars in cash through the mail in the course of two weeks and the same could happen to you if you just send a ten-dollar bill to the last person on the list and mail out a couple of dozen letters of your own. Don't be fooled.

Con jobs like this are often referred to as "pyramid schemes." The people who start them may rake in the money, but the further down the list you are, the more likely it is that you'll simply be robbed. For most of us, it would be more accurate to think of such schemes in terms of rivers flowing backward. The money goes to the previous person on the list. And since rivers don't naturally flow backward, at some point they are going to turn into dry creeks. That will probably be at the point when you fork over your money.

As to the faith letters, which recount glowing tales of good luck that has come to those who sent out copies, and dire stories of death and destruction that have befallen those who didn't, all you have to do is read the prose. Any bright fifth-grader would start off by correcting the grammar. Perhaps because he played Moses, Charlton Heston's name almost invariably crops up in these letters. The authors would have you believe that his career went into a decline because he didn't take the trouble to send this junk on to such pals as Ronald Reagan.

Actually, Mr. Heston seems to be doing rather well. And so will you if you throw any chain letter you receive, whether it involves money or faith, into the wastebasket immediately. Of course, there's nothing wrong with having a good chuckle first.

CHAMPAGNE CORKS

It's a festive occasion—New Year's Eve, a wedding anniversary, or the day you won the lottery. Champagne is in order. You remove the wires over the cork and the protective foil. Now you place your thumbs on either side of the cork and begin easing it out. Suddenly, with a loud pop, the cork shoots across the room and everybody cheers. Everybody would do better to duck.

A champagne bottle should never be opened in the manner described above, fun though it may seem. Why not? Because it has been estimated that a champagne cork shoots out of the bottle at a speed of more than 40 feet per second. Think what could happen if that exploding cork hit someone in the mouth or an eye. Such injuries are in fact quite common and can be serious.

The proper way to open a champagne bottle, according to numerous wine experts, is to place one hand *over* the cork, gripping firmly, while turning the *bottle* itself with the other hand, placed around the neck of the bottle. Aside from avoiding accidents, you'll get the cork out more easily using this technique. It also makes it possible to pour the champagne quickly if it should overflow. It should be noted, however, that a rapid overflow means the champagne is too cold, with a resulting loss of flavor. A temperature of 35 to 40 degrees is regarded as ideal.

CHANGING YOUR NAME

In the film *Beat The Devil*, written by Truman Capote and directed by John Huston, Peter Lorre plays a suspicious character named O'Hara. Another character finds this a peculiar moniker, and asks about it. In his heavy German accent, Peter Lorre replies, "There are many Germans with Irish names living in Brazil."

Few of us have quite so sinister a reason for wanting to change our names, but nonetheless namechanging is a very common occurrence in the United States. Many immigrants have shortened or changed their names to make them more congruent with English pronunciation. Politicians may change their names for reasons lost in the mists of time or prevarication, as in Senator Gary Hart's decision to become Hart instead of Hartpence when he was in his twenties. Actors are often forced to change their names, either for aesthetic reasons, as in the case of Archie Leach becoming Cary Grant, or because their real names are already "taken," as in one James Stewart becoming Stewart Granger.

You can go to court and have your name legally changed, but you needn't always undertake that trouble and expense. Banks, for example, will honor checks made out to either your real name or your pseudonym, provided you go in person to inform them of the situation and your reasons for it and have both names listed on your signature card. In bureaucratic terms, the easiest solution is usually to have a "joint" account in both names. When it comes to the IRS, however, you will have to decide which name to file under and make sure that any checks paid you are issued in that name. If you wish to use a new name, you must apply for a new Social Security number and have all checks made out to the adopted name. The IRS is not prepared to deal with split personalities—after all, you could considerably lower your taxes by filing half your income under one name and half under the other.

CHOKING FITS

Everyone should know how to perform the Heimlich maneuver. If a person is choking on food or some object that has been inadvertently swallowed, stand behind the victim and wrap your arms around the person above the waist. Make a fist of one hand and place it just below the center of the rib cage, with the large knuckle of the thumb pressed inward. Cover the fist with your other hand and thrust it inward and upward several times. The lodged food or object should pop upward out of the windpipe.

Some medical dictionaries and first-aid brochures continue to recommend that you slap the victim's back between the shoulder blades before performing the Heimlich maneuver, but Dr. Heimlich strongly disagrees. Slapping the back may cause the lodged food to descend further own the windpipe. Stick with the Heimlich maneuver; it has already saved the lives of countless people, including Mayor Koch of New York.

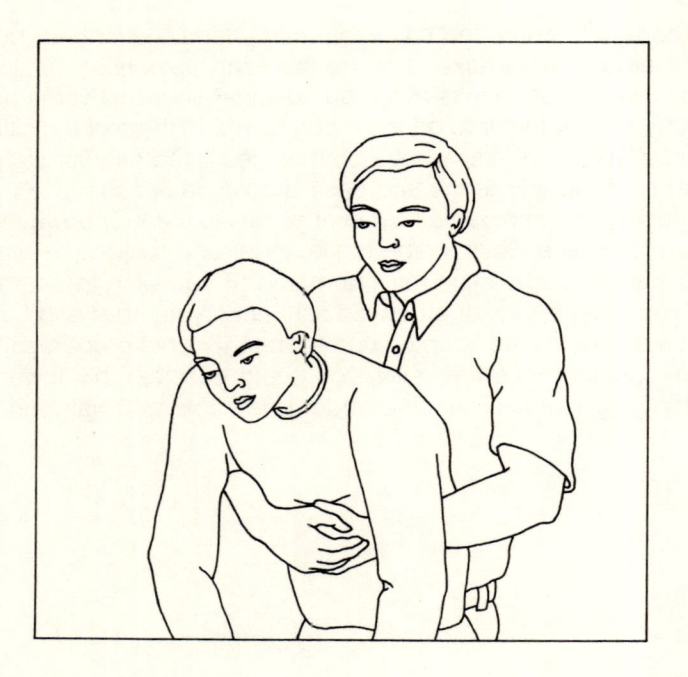

CLAM DIGGING

At low tide, when the sandbars rise like islands, you will see the clam diggers with their rakes and pails, seeking the succulent mollusks burrowing in the sand. Some don't even bother with rakes; they use their feet to dislodge the clams. Clam digging, a search for edible buried treasure, is an activity that children as well as adults can delight in.

But a few warnings are in order. Before going clamming, you should always check with local health authorities to make sure that the clams are safe to eat. Clams are easily affected by environmental factors and can become toxic as a result of man-made pollution or the presence of "red tide," caused by the proliferation of a noxious plankton.

Be on the lookout for razor clams, which are found on both the East and West Coasts; they make delectable chowder and provide a special challenge because they are difficult to harvest. They advertise their presence by small holes in the wet sand, and their shells are as sharp as their name. You have to dig for razor clams with a shovel, because they burrow deeper in the direction of the sea at an astonishing speed. Facing the sea, thrust the shovel in to a depth of about five inches and turn the sand over. If you've been quick enough, you've got the beginnings of a superior meal.

Razor clams, like soft-shell and bar clams, are very sandy. To remove the grit, place them in a bucket of seawater or salted fresh water, add a cup of cornmeal, and let them rest for several hours. The clams will absorb the cornmeal, making them more tender, and expel the sand. Good eating!

CLOTHING ALTERATIONS

Free Alterations!

That means you can buy clothing that doesn't fit, and the store will fix everything up for you at no extra cost.

Beware.

Listen to a retired garment industry executive who prefers to remain anonymous:

"If it's a matter of raising or lowering the hem of a skirt, or tailoring unhemmed trousers to your exact height, that's a legitimate alteration and a real service. But beyond that, you should think twice, maybe three times. Free alterations are a way of selling people clothes they really shouldn't be buying. Women are pretty smart about this, but men can be real dunces. The clerk says, 'That suit really looks good on you, Sir. All we need to do is take in the seat of the trousers a little, and smooth things out at the back of the jacket so it doesn't bunch up between your shoulders.' Take my word for it, if they have to do that, the suit doesn't belong on your body in the first place. If you really like the suit, and you think it might be fixable, say, Okay, but I'm not going to pay for it until I see how the alterations come out. That'll cut off the sales pitch in a hurry, unless the clerk really thinks it can be properly altered."

Think twice, maybe three times. That's the right way.

COFFEE FLAVOR

The citizens of New Orleans, Louisiana are convinced that they make the best coffee in the world, and there are many coffee connoisseurs who agree. It is true that New Orleans cooks often add chicory to their coffee, but even if you do not like the flavor of chicory, you can make stronger, fresher, brighter-tasting coffee by following the New Orleans technique.

The secret lies in adding water a little at a time. A drip pot with a filter is the best and easiest kind to use when employing this technique. Measure the desired amount of coffee into the filter, and then bring to a boil the necessary amount of water. Initially, add only a few tablespoons of the boiling water to the coffee grounds, and let them swell for five minutes. Then pour in one-third of the remaining water, brought once again to the boil. Repeat two more times. Because the coffee grounds swell more each time you pour the water in, the coffee drips through much more slowly, and additional flavor is extracted. This may sound like a lot of trouble, but you can do it while you are making dinner, and the resulting intensity of flavor will be more than worth the effort.

COMMON COLDS

More horseradish (which can, incidentally, help to unclog the sinuses) has been written about the common cold than perhaps any other subject. The common cold is ubiquitous, and since no one is immune, everyone can claim expertise. Does eating chocolate or hard candy increase the likelihood of catching a cold? That is one theory, based on the premise that sticky, sugary substances irritate the mucous membranes and leave them exposed to infection. Can massive doses of vitamin A or vitamin C prevent colds or stop them dead in their tracks? People argue the pros and cons of that issue as virulently as any cold that ever raged through their systems. Will chicken soup, herbal teas, or acupuncture speed your recovery? How about trying the classic nineteenth-century remedy of hanging a hat on the bedpost, drinking whiskey until you see two hats, and then going to sleep?

In this morass, there are a few *facts* to note. There are at least 200 different viruses and/or bacteria that can cause the infection. That's why it is so difficult to find a "cure" and why so many theories abound. However, a few things have been established; for example, wet feet will not increase your chances of getting a cold, but fatigue will. Psychological factors may indeed be involved. Studies made by Great Britain's prestigious Common Cold Unit indicate that introverts get worse colds than extroverts.

Some of the established facts are curious. Male babies under three years of age are more likely to get colds than females; but after that age, boys are less affected and girls more so. No one really knows why this should be the case, except that male infants generally suffer more health problems than female infants. It is true that chicken soup helps to relieve cold symptoms; but it is only marginally more effective than plain hot water. It's the heat that's important, because it acts to clear nasal passages.

Discouragingly, there are virtually no drugs used to treat colds that do not have at least minor side effects in some people, ranging from stomach irritation to dizziness. Many drugs can have serious side effects, especially for people suffering from other medical problems such as diabetes or high blood pressure.

The wrong way to treat a cold is to stuff yourself full of pills and try to keep going. You'll probably prolong your misery, at best, and may even develop complications like pneumonia.

The right way is as old as common sense. Get plenty of rest, keep warm, and drink lots of liquids, preferably hot. Some things just don't change.

COMPOST PILING

A compost pile is not just a heap of garden detritus. It is a technique for creating useful fertilizer for your soil, and as such it requires attention both to its composition and its ongoing care. According to Joan Lee Faust, author of *The New York Times Book of Vegetable Gardening*, "Most compost professionals recommend a mix of two-thirds carbonaceous material to one-third nitrogenous material. Carbonaceous materials would include straw, spoiled hay, autumn leaves, wood chips, sawdust, chopped cornstalks, pine needles, and shredded newspaper. Nitrogenous materials include spent annual and vegetable plants, grass clippings, kitchen vegetable waste materials, weeds, manures (fresh or dried) and soil layers."

All gardening experts advise adding a high nitrogen fertilizer to the various layers of a compost pile as it is built up to speed decomposition. At the bottom of the pile, put a layer of twigs to assure that the compost will be well aerated. Then add carbonaceous material, a layer of nitrogenous material half as thick, sprinkle with fertilizer, top with a one-inch layer of good soil, and repeat the process until the pile is four to five feet tall.

There should be a depression at the center of the pile, so that it will collect water. You can surround tte compost pile with chicken wire or concrete blocks, which gives a neater appearance, but this is not essential. While a compost pile will rot even if left undisturbed, many experts recommend turning it once a month with a pitchfork. Turning is necessary if you wish to continue adding such kitchen scraps as eggshells, coffee grounds, and vegetable trimmings. Do not add meat scraps, as they may cause offensive odors. If you start a compost pile in the fall it should be ready for use as fertilizer the following spring.

CONTEST CHOICES

The advertisements arrive on a regular basis: Sweepstakes! Grand Prize $250,000. Or it may be a new house, a fancy sports car, a mink coat. All you have to do is return your entry blank. "You can't win if you don't enter!" You probably can't win if you do, either. In one 1984 national magazine sweepstakes, for example, your chances of winning even a *third* prize were one in 16,975,500. But it is tempting because people do win.

If you are tempted enough to enter the contest, you'll probably also be inclined to agree to subscribe to the magazine, accept the merchandise, donate to the charity, or whatever. By law, you must be informed that no purchase is necessary to enter. It may seem pretty certain to you, nonetheless, that unless you make a purchase, you'll never win the contest. Why else do they give you two separate contest forms, and sometimes two separate envelopes—one simply to enter the sweepstakes and the other to accept the product *and* enter the contest.

The reason you are given two separate forms or envelopes is partially a practical one: it helps speed the processing of the orders that do come in. But is also has a psychological effect, nudging you toward saying YES. Many people simply will not believe that they have just as good a chance of winning if they say NO to the offer.

But that's wrong. Studies of some sweepstakes have shown, in fact, that by the luck of the draw, there have been more NO winners than YES winners.

So don't let yourself be brainwashed into buying merchandise you don't really want. In some things, a NO is just as good as a YES.

CONVULSIONS

Convulsions, in the form of a grand mal seizure, are commonly associated with epilepsy. The person falls to the ground; breathing may cease momentarily and then resume with heavy rasping as the lungs begin to function again. The person's limbs are likely to jerk spasmodically, and copious amounts of saliva, often of a foamy consistency, will be spewed from the mouth.

It is a frightening sight, and as a result, bystanders often overreact. They may try to hold the person down or attempt to bring him or her out of the seizure. This is the wrong approach, according to experts in the field, including those involved in ongoing research at the University of Virginia. There is nothing that can be done to prevent a grand mal seizure from running its course or to hasten its conclusion. It can be helpful to loosen clothing, especially a tight collar. A pillow or coat placed beneath the head can prevent the victim from banging it against the floor during severe convulsions. Some experts advise turning the person on his or her side in order to facilitate the flow of saliva (which is by the way a *healthy* body reaction and not a sign of dementia). There is some disagreement among experts as to whether or not to insert anything into the victim's mouth. Some are against it because it can impede the flow of saliva; others believe that the insertion of a soft object such as a soft glasses case can prevent biting of the tongue. All agree, however, that no hard object should be inserted.

Should you call for an ambulance to have the victim taken to a hospital? In most cases, that isn't necessary. Unless he or she has been hurt in falling, or undergoes a continuing series of seizures, all that is needed after consciousness is regained is rest and quiet. Don't be alarmed if the person seems somewhat disoriented at first and cannot remember what has happened. This is invariably the case.

Grand mal seizures are not always a sign of epilepsy per se. They can be brought on by excessive fatigue (they have been known to occur, for example, in college students who have had little sleep for several days while cramming for exams), or they can be the result of alcohol withdrawal. Seizures can also be brought on by an allergic reaction to a drug or a drug overdose—in these cases hospitalization is necessary.

The exact causes of such seizures and of epilepsy are still not fully understood, although we do know that an abnormal electrical discharge in the brain is involved. Fortunately, a number of drugs have been developed that can bring the seizures under control, the most commonly prescribed being Dilantin. Thanks to such drugs, even chronic epileptics can lead perfectly normal lives.

CREDIT ESTABLISHMENT

Many people believe that the more money you make, the more credit you can get. But it doesn't really work that way. It is true that if you have a low income it will be more difficult to establish credit, but you can also have a very good income and have difficulty in getting a large loan—for a mortgage, say—unless the credit bureaus or the bank can be provided with evidence that you have a history of paying your debts as they come due. Credit officers, to put it simply, are more interested in your track record than ii your income. It you've incurred debts and paid them off on time you'll be a more attractive credit risk than someone who has never had any debts. This may sound peculiar—indeed there are economists who believe that it is not only peculiar but dangerous to the solvency of the whole country—but that is the American way.

Thus, if you are just starting out in the world of credit, the best thing you can do is incur a small debt. Borrow a nominal sum, say $500, from your company's credit union or from a bank, even if you don't need it, and then pay it off. You are now on your way.

There is a story about a famous actress who, many years ago, asked her husband for a fur coat. He said they couldn't afford it, that he was $20,000 in debt as it was. She replied, "A man of your talents ought to be at least $100,000 in debt." Strangely enough, financial institutions take much the same view—after all, they make their money because people are in debt.

CROSSWORD QUANDARIES

Riding public transportation, sitting in a waiting room, or having lunch at a coffee shop, you see someone else at it: doing a crossword puzzle in *ink*. Infuriating!

You telephone friends on a Sunday afternoon. You've already spent an hour on the crossword puzzle, making very little progress. "Oh," they say, "we finished that before brunch." Maddening!

And then, in the puzzles themselves, there are all thooe Ethiopian antelopes leaping about, not to mention Amazonian birds, cawing derisively. You ran up against these obscure fauna a couple of months ago, you realize, but you haven't an inkling as to what they're called. And what on earth was that New Guinea port that keeps cropping up?

The definition is *Carpenter's friend*. Let's see. Hammer. Maybe. Vise, awl, screwdriver, no, no, no, this isn't going anywhere. Another tack. Carpenter. Carleton Carpenter, of "Abba-dabba Honeymoon?" Friend. Debbie Reynolds. NO. Your mind is beginning to skid. Wait a minute. Walrus. "The Walrus and the Carpenter" from *Alice's Adventures in Wonderland*. "Soup of the Evening." How very clever. How very annoying.

Face it, crossword puzzles are an Alice-in-Wonderland world, and if you have the right kind of twisted mind, you'll be very good at them. More power to you. But if you don't, yet still enjoy the challenge, get yourself a comprehensive crossword dictionary, and look up those damn antelopes, every time.

And don't let anybody tell you that's wrong. In some endeavors, cheating is the only way out.

CUSTOMS CUES

In a period of less than three months, two rock stars and two movie stars get nabbed at London's Heathrow Airport, trying to smuggle drugs past customs agents. How stupid can they be, you think. Do they think they can get away with anything, just because they're famous?

On the other hand, your cousin Marjorie proudly relates how she managed to sneak that diamond watch she bought in Switzerland past U.S. Customs without paying a dime in duty. Now that, you think, is pretty clever; we all pay too many taxes as it is.

All right, there is a difference between illegal substances and trying to dodge a tax, but it is a difference in degree, not kind. In both cases, what has transpired is against the law. If Marjorie had been caught, not only would she have had to pay the duty, she could also have been fined. What's more, when customs agents find one infraction, they immediately start looking for more. You can be delayed for several humiliating hours. Some foreign countries will send you right back where you came from. Others will arrest you on the spot.

The wrong way to deal with customs, anywhere in the world, is to play games. Declare the goods that must be declared, pay your duty tax and forget the drugs.

If you have to carry a hypodermic needle because you are a diabetic or for any other medical reason, always have a letter from your doctor with you. And always carry prescription pills in their original bottle, with the pharmacist's label on it. Customs agents don't trust anybody, and with good reason.

CUT-RATE FARES

The deregulation of the airline industry in 1980 created temporary chaos in the travel business. The airlines began changing fares and even routes from day to day, making it impossible for even large travel agencies to keep up with what was happening or to pass on to their customers the economies and greater convenience that were supposed to result from deregulation. Matters have settled down considerably, but the traveler may still have to do some persistent digging to take advantage of the lowest fares.

One of the roadblocks is an ingenious computerized runaround used by many of the major airlines to increase the likelihood that you will fly with them and not with a competitor. When you call most airlines to ascertain what flights are available, and at what cost, the first two or even three screens that appear on the ticket agent's computer focus on that company's own flights. There may be a flight on another airline that is scheduled to depart in between two of the flights that initially appear, or a flight at a lower cost, but the agent will have to go through several more screens to find them. The information is there, but it's buried, and it will take time to dig it out. If you have the time, it can be well worth your while to insist that the agent make the effort to accommodate you. After all, deregulation was intended to be good for the consumer, not just the airlines.

Be persistent and save yourself some money.

DEATH ANNOUNCEMENTS

The major national newspapers keep obituary files on famous people that are constantly updated and rewritten. If a major figure dies, the obituary can be "pulled" from the file, a paragraph added on the circumstances of death, and the piece will be ready to go to press in minutes. Files are also kept on less well-known but distinguished citizens. Whether an obituary runs on the first page of a newspaper, in another section, or is relegated on to the obituary page itself is strictly an editorial decision, usually based on how "important" the person was during his lifetime.

If you'd like to record in the newspaper the death of a dear friend or relative who would not ordinarily receive a news story or obituary, you can do so by paying. Many newspapers have columns recording death announcements, which are treated in the same way as any other classified ad. The sum you pay can vary considerably according to the importance and circulation of the newspaper. It may be a nominal sum in a newspaper in a small city. *The New York Times*, as of this writing, charges $10.20 a line for weekday editions.

If you are calling in a death announcement, write it out in full first, and read the copy to the newspaper. You will be sent a bill through the mail.

DEBT MANAGEMENT

Several bills are three or more months overdue. Your creditors are telephoning you at home, demanding payment and threatening to take you to court. You simply don't have the money to pay your debts, and you are far too overextended to qualify for additional loans. It looks as though the only answer is to file for bankruptcy.

Before you do that, try another avenue. There are hundreds of credit counseling services across the country that may be able to help you to work out long-term repayment schedules with your creditors and stop them from harassing you. Large numbers of these services are staffed by volunteers and are free. If there is no listing for Consumer Credit Counseling in your local telephone book, see if your city's Consumer Affairs Department can give you a referral. Or you can write to the National Foundation for Consumer Credit at 1819 H Street, NW, Washington, D.C. 20006.

You should be prepared to give up your credit cards as part of the process of getting out of debt. But you'd lose them if you declared bankruptcy anyway. At least investigate the possibility of taking an intermediate step toward solvency instead of the drastic one of bankruptcy.

DIAMOND DUPLICITIES

Diamonds may be beautiful, and virtually indestructible, but it's highly doubtful whether they are a girl's best friend—at least in the way suggested by the famous song. As an investment, small diamonds are not a reliable hedge against inflation, according to experts. Any diamond under a carat will bring about a quarter of what was originally paid for it. In order to be quite certain that your diamond will rise in value, it has to be large enough, or have a sufficiently distinguished provenance (i.e., was once owned by Catherine the Great or some such famous person) to cost you $20,000 or up to begin with.

Give diamonds for love, and buy them only at stores with impeccable reputations. Artificial diamonds are often of such high quality these days that only an expert can tell them from the real thing. If you think you're getting a bargain, you're probably getting a fake.

DIET PILLS

Every year millions of Americans, in their efforts to lose weight, purchase over-thh-counter diet pills that are claimed to suppress the appetite. Doctors have questioned whether they actually do that or not ever since they first appeared on the market. It's been widely suggested that they have a placebo effect—that is, the person taking them expects them to reduce hunger pangs and therefore persuades himself or herself that an afternoon snack isn't needed. But recently, a far more serious question has been raised: are they safe?

A common and mistaken assumption of American consumers is that if a drug is sold over-the-counter at the local drugstore, there can be no danger in taking it. If there were any doubts, the drug would be sold only by prescription. Unfortunately, that simply isn't true.

Diet pills illustrate this point. Most brands carry a warning on the label stating that the drug should not be taken if you have high blood pressure, heart, thyroid, or kidney disease or if you're pregnant. Well, you're not pregnant and you don't have any of those other medical problems, so why worry? One reason to worry is that public health officials, on every level from local to federal, have estimated that as many as 40 percent of people with high blood pressure *don't know they have it*. When was the last time you had your blood pressure checked? Even more alarming, evidence has been presented before Congress that some women who took diet pills in the early stages of pregnancy—before they realized they were pregnant—have given birth to children with birth defects.

So don't make automatic assumptions about the safety of over-the-counter pills. Especially if it's a drug you haven't taken before, read and consider any warning labels carefully. Are you *sure* you don't have high blood pressure? Have you been trying to get pregnant? The safety of drugs should never be taken for granted.

DEFROSTING REFRIGERATORS

Refrigerator defrosting is one of the messiest of kitchen chores. Although modern refrigerators are ostensibly "frost-free," layers of ice can build up even in them if the freezer door is opened and closed excessively. And there are many older refrigerators still in use, especially in rental apartments in urban areas, which require periodic defrosting.

There are three things you can do to reduce frost buildup and make defrosting less of a problem. First, keep the freezing compartment throughly filled. The less air space there is in the compartment, the less condensation there will be to build up on the walls of the compartment. If you don't keep frozen foods on hand in quantity, then fill the empty space with plastic bags packed with ice.

Open the freezer door as seldom as possible. Think what you are going to need in the course of preparing a meal, and take all the items out at once. If you or your family uses a lot of ice, an automatic icemaker may be a good investment in the long run, since every time you open the freezer door, an additional surge of electricity is needed to maintain the temperature.

Third, never let the ice buildup on the walls of the compartment exceed a quarter inch. Not only is it much easier and faster to defrost a thin coating, but a thick coating will interfere with your refrigerator's efficiency, requiring additional electricity usage, and hastening further buildup. You may have to defrost more often, but it will be a much less nasty job and save you money.

Unhappily, putting pans of hot water in the compartment remains the fastest method of defrosting. Once you've put the pan in, close the freezer door. Leaving the door to the compartment open will only slow down the process, since much of the heat from the pans will escape into the air of the room. A hair dryer can be useful for melting large chunks of ice, if you've let things get that far out of hand.

Never use any sharp object to chip away at the ice. Not only do you run the risk of puncturing the cooling system, but also of breaking off the end of a good knife.

DOG BONES

Dogs love bones. They grind away at them with utter concentration. They bury them in the garden and stash them under beds. You think you're doing your dog a favor when you toss it a bone. But many veterinarians, including Terri McGinnis, author of *The Well Dog Book*, suggest you think twice.

There's no doubt that bones help satisfy a dog's chewing urge. Better than my slipper, you may think. Chewing a bone also helps clean a dog's teeth, but rawhide chews have the same effect and cause less wear on the teeth. The real problem arises, though, when a dog starts to *eat* a bone. A dog that eats a bone (including a rawhide chew) may get gastritis, constipation, or throw it all up on your living room rug. Bones that splinter easily, such as poultry bones, pork chop bones, and even steak bones, can perforate your dog's intestines.

Because they are very hard, marrow bones and knucklebones are most recommended by veterinarians for chewing. A dog can chew on such bones for an hour and produce only shavings. But, as Terri McGinnis says, "If you see that your dog is *eating* a bone, take it away." Safest of all are fake bones made of molded nylon: they are impossible to eat.

DRUG STORAGE

According to the Food and Drug Administration, cases of accidental drug overdose among children have declined 60 percent since 1968. This decline is largely the result of the introduction of "child-proof" caps on both prescription and nonprescription drugs. But problems remain. Not all drugs are required to have such caps to begin with. Even when such caps are present, many children are remarkably clever at getting them off. (Think of all those seven-year-old whizzes putting a Rubiks Cube back into proper alignment.)

Also, because many elderly people (or just plain adults, for that matter) have trouble opening child-proof caps, screw caps remain available by request for many drugs. Or a person with arthritis, for instance, may transfer a drug to a more easily opened container. And then the grandchildren come for a visit.

On account of all these factors, it remains vital to keep any and all drugs out of reach of children. And that means *really* out of reach. Could your child stand on a chair and get at them? Then they are not out of reach. If necessary, lock the drugs up.

EAR PIERCING

The wrong way to get your ears pierced is to go to anybody but an accredited physician. "Ears pierced on the premises," when the premises are anything but a doctor's office can lead to piercing pain when infection sets in a day or two later.

ECLIPSE VIEWING

From the beginning of human history humankind has regarded the solar eclipse as the most spectacular celestial event. In many ancient societies, solar eclipses were viewed not only with awe but also with fear, often regarded as a portent of the end of the world—indeed, such fears persist to this day among certain primitive peoples. Over the past century, of course, astronomers have learned to predict solar eclipses to the day decades in advance. But while we have put superstition behind us, there is still good reason to exercise great care when viewing a solar eclipse.

Professor Donald H. Menzel, author of *Astronomy*, spells out the dangers: "Many persons—especially children—tend to stare directly into the sun during an eclipse and may sustain severe burns of the retina. In such a situation the lens of the eye acts like a magnifying glass, focussing the sun's light upon the retina and burning it, sometimes severely enough to cause blindness."

What is the right way to view an eclipse? Dr. Menzel and other experts suggest a variety of techniques for safe viewing. Welder's goggles are probably best for direct viewing. You can also protect your eyes with a large piece of photographic film—such as an x-ray negative—developed until it is almost black, or a sheet of glass heavily smoked on both sides in a candle flame. Neither of these is absolutely safe, however. The safest way is to settle for an indirect view using a simple homemade device. Punch a hole an eighth of an inch in diameter in a large piece of cardboard. During the eclipse, the cardboard should be held several feet above the ground. The light coming through the hole will be focused, and the progress of the eclipse can be viewed on the ground where the light hits it.

If the eclipse is total, it is safe to look directly at the sun for the brief period of totality. At that time the black disk of the moon will block out all sunlight except for the magnificent corona, and the light will be of approximately the same brilliance as that of a full moon. As soon as the sun begins to reappear, however, the initial viewing precautions must be taken again.

EGG BOILING

The old joke about the young wife who "doesn't even know how to boil an egg" is unfair to new brides. A lot of experienced cooks have problems with boiled eggs, too. There are eggs that crack while cooking, soft-boiled eggs with hardened yolks, and hard-boiled eggs that won't peel properly or have a discolored greenish line around the edges of the yolk.

Perhaps because the subject is not simple and is surrounded by controversy, many cookbooks avoid the issue altogether. "Boil an egg," they say. But M.F.K. Fisher gave the subject her usual witty attention in *How to Cook a Wolf,* and Julia Child once devoted an entire half-hour television program to the mysteries of boiling an egg, information subsequently published in *From Julia Child's Kitchen.*

There are many issues hotly debated by egg fanciers.

Should the eggs be brought to room temperature before they are boiled? Some say that helps to prevent cracking; others disagree. There is no question, however, that an egg straight from a cold refrigerator will have to be cooked for a minute or two longer.

Does punching a pinhole in the large end of the egg prevent cracking? Mrs. Fisher is dubious; Mrs. Child insists on it.

Should the eggs be started in cold water or dropped (carefully) into already boiling water? There are disagreements among chefs in this area, also.

But there is one thing that everyone agrees on. No egg should ever actually be *boiled*. It must be *simmered*. Boiling an egg will make the white tough. The boiling water will bounce the egg around and may crack it. And excess heat causes the yolk to discolor.

Turn the heat down. SIMMER. And you'll get a superior "boiled egg."

EGGSTEROL

You are worried about the cholesterol in your diet. Therefore you've cut back sharply on your consumption of eggs or tried to eliminate them altogether from your diet. That's one of the best steps you could take to control the cholesterol in your body, and prevent the buildup of the plaque that causes hardening of the arteries. Right?

Not necessarily.

This is a very controversial area, so let's start with a few facts. First, cholesterol is manufactured within your body every day, primarily by your liver but also by other organs. If your intake of cholesterol in food falls below certain levels, your body will compensate by metabolizing it from other materials. It can even turn carbohydrates into cholesterol.

The reason your body is so busy manufacturing cholesterol is that it is essential to human life, especially vital to the brain, liver, nerves, and blood. It even forms the nucleus of your sex hormones!

But what about preventing hardening of the arteries? First of all, it has never been proved that an "excess" of cholesterol causes the buildup of plaque in the arteries. In fact, up-to-date medical textbooks explain that researchers are still not certain of the mechanisms that create those deposits. Certain studies have deduced that cholesterol is the villain, but all such studies have been called into question by other researchers and physicians.

Even if you've been convinced that cholesterol is the villain, you should still think twice about avoiding eggs. For one thing, eggs contain not only cholesterol but also lecithin in considerable amounts. Lecithin is an emulsifier that helps cholesterol dissolve in the blood. Don't, however, rush out and buy commercial lecithin products to take as a dietary supplement, as some "health" food proselytizers suggest. There's abundant lecithin in a normal diet. There's also as much controversy about how lecithin really works as there is about cholesterol itself.

But they are both present in eggs, and since those who preach against eggs are usually pro lecithin, their argument is neutralized. More important, eggs are one of the best natural sources of protein and other nutrients available to us.

If you're still doubtful, consider that even Dr. Michael Debakey, the pioneering heart surgeon from Houston, is on record as approving the inclusion of eggs in the normal diet.

ELECTRICAL PLUGGING

The wall outlet is loose, and you have to balance the plug just right or the lamp keeps going out. The kitchen counter outlet gives off sparks when you plug or unplug the toaster or the food processor.

Many people ignore such problems at the risk of serious injury from an electric shock or the possibility of fire. Wall outlets eventually wear out, and they should be replaced as soon as a problem becomes evident. This is a task that can be carried out by the home handyman with some knowledge of electrical wiring. There are numerous home repair books, such as *Reader's Digest Fix-It Yourself Manual*, that give thorough instructions for such repair work. The actual work itself is not that difficult, but you are warned to make absolutely sure that the current is off. For this you'll need a voltage tester. No electrician would undertake such a job without using a voltage tester at the site of the repair. This inexpensive tool makes it possible to double-check the safety of proceeding—necessary because in some cases one half of a room may be on one circuit, while the other half is fed through another.

If you have any doubts whatsoever about your ability to make an electrical repair job, call a professional, right away.

ELEVATOR BREAKDOWNS

Many people don't like elevators to begin with. They find them claustrophobic, and they get extremely queasy when an elevator leaps up or down twenty floors at a bound in skyscrapers. The very thought of being trapped inside a stalled elevator gives such people nightmares. Unfortunately, it does happen, and more frequently than either passengers, building managers, or elevator companies would like. If it happens to you, the worst thing you can possibly do, no matter how much you hate elevators, is to panic and try to effect your own rescue.

Safety requirements for elevators have become much more stringent in recent years, but there are still many old elevators in use that give the appearance of being easy to escape from. You may be tempted to hoist yourself through a trapdoor in the roof of the car or pry open the metal gates (as opposed to solid doors on newer elevators) and climb up or down to the next floor. But consider the famous cases of the disasters that have resulted from such maneuvers. The actor Pat Hingle lost two fingers of one hand in such an attempt; the great exponent of Gilbert and Sullivan patter songs, Martyn Green, had a leg so badly crushed that it had to be amputated. The problem is that if someone is trying to get the elevator moving again and it starts up while you are outside the "cage," you could be very seriously injured.

Push the alarm button, and wait to be rescued. Even it you don't hear the alarm go off, stay put. Eventually someone will realize that your elevator is out of order and will investigate. Pounding on an elevator door or yelling should only be done at well-spaced intervals, because such physical exertion will use up the air in a sealed elevator more quickly.

During the November 1965 blackout in New York City, it was subsequently reported in the press, a number of people were trapped in an elevator on a high floor of the Empire State Building. More than a hour went by before firemen reached the floor by the emergency stairs. They pounded on the door, and called out, "Are they any pregnant women in there?"

A muffled male voice replied, "Give us time, we've only begun to get acquainted."

Now that's the spirit in which to deal with an elevator breakdown.

ENGINE REPAIRS

If you hear your car making peculiar sounds and suspect that something is wrong with the engine, don't wait until it stalls in traffic, boils over on the highway, or fails to start one morning. Get it checked.

BUT, AND THIS IS A VERY BIG BUT, don't let a loose wire, faulty spark plug, or worn radiator hose escalate into a $300 repair job. There are many small problems, inexpensive to fix, which can cause your car to make strange sounds. There are also, unfortunately, many garage mechanics who have never heard of the old saying, "If it ain't broke, don't fix it." Some will even make sure it does get broken.

Consumer agencies suggest several ways you can protect yourself from being taken.

1. Before going to a mechanic, try to arrive at some idea on your own as to what is wrong with your car. If you are one of those people who has no conception of what goes on under the hood or how the various automobile systems work, you are asking to be gypped. Get a simple layman's manual and at least familiarize yourself with the basics.
2. Always ask for a written estimate from the garage. If the mechanic refuses to give you one, go elsewhere.
3. A mechanic may, in the course of the repair work, discover some other incipient problem that should be taken care of. But request that he or she telephone you if any other problems come up or if it is discovered that the repair job is going to cost more than the estimate. That way, you have an opportunity to say no. Again, if the mechanic doesn't comply with the request to call you, go elsewhere next time.
4. When you pick up your car, ask for a written guarantee covering the work that has been done. The guarantee may only cover a short period—say 30 days—but even that can save you money if the engine still isn't running properly.
5. Also ask for the parts that were taken out of your car and replaced. This is another way of keeping the mechanic honest; and even a worn part might come in handy in an emergency situation on the road.

ESCALATOR ETIQUETTE

You're in a big department store. The elevators are crowded and slow and you have shopping to do on several floors, so you take the escalators. Thinking about your purchases, you lose track of what floor you're on and you take one step off the escalator and stop to check the signs. You'd better not. There are people behind you, being carried inevitably forward. Unless you keep moving forward, too, the people are going to be carried into you and crash; somebody behind you could fall.

Escalator accidents are one of the major safety concerns of department store security forces. They recommend—no, beg—that when you reach the top of an escalator, you take at least ten paces forward before stopping to look around.

Most escalator accidents involve the elderly, who may have a problem stepping onto or off of the moving stairs quickly enough, and young children who get a shoelace or a pant leg or the tip of a sandal caught in the mechanism. If you're with an elderly person who is tentative on escalators, take his or her arm at the top and keep moving forward. Better yet, take an elevator if it's available. When you've got kids in tow, check them out. Are those shoelaces tied? Teach them that they have to stand still and pay attention on an escalator. Escalators are neither a private limousine nor a merry-go-round. They're a way of moving as many people through a store as quickly as possible. That means pay attention and step lively.

ESCAPING A HOTEL FIRE

Several major hotel fires in recent years have alerted the public to the dangers of being trapped in an unfamiliar high-rise hotel, or a motel with only a few stories but containing sealed windows and a confusing maze of corridors. Yet many people fail to take the precautions they should to protect their lives in case of fire.

J. Brooks Semple, one of the foremost experts on hotel safety, offers a number of recommendations. When you check into a hotel, the first thing you should do is to take stock of the safety situation. Is there an instruction sheet in your room, telling you what to do in case of fire? If not, call the desk and ask for one. Even if there is a sheet, and you find it difficult to comprehend, call the desk and ask about any points that puzzle you. Is there a smoke detector in your room? If not, call the desk and ask why not. Check the windows of your room. Are they sealed? You may want to request a change in rooms, or even to change hotels. (Several airlines will not permit their personnel to stay in a room with sealed windows.)

Does this sound excessively cautious? Are you concerned about making a nuisance of yourself with the front desk? Stop and consider that it's a matter of your personal safety—and possibly your life. Mr. Semple notes that while many hotels are taking active steps to increase safety, others remain laggard. The more inquiries they get about fire safety, the more lives may be saved.

A further step you can take to protect yourself is to investigate the emergency exits. Leave your room and count the number of doors to the nearest emergency stairway exit. Go through the exit and, keeping the door propped open with your foot, check to see if the door is locked from the other side. It may be locked for security reasons—but it should not be locked in case of a fire emergency. Complain about it. If there is a fire, you might go through such a doorway, let it close behind you, and find that the stairwell is filled with smoke and you're trapped.

You should also determine how many flights of stairs you would have to go down in order to reach the outside. Are you worried about how far down you'll have to go? Ask for a room on a lower floor.

Now you've taken all the precautions you can. But what should you do in case a fire does break out?

Go to the door of your room and feel it. If it is hot, stay where you are. If it is cool, open it and check the amount of smoke in the corridor. If there is little or no smoke, head for that emergency stairwell exit (never the elevator). *Don't forget to take your room key with you.* You might reach the stairwell and find it impassable, in which case the safest thing to do is to return to your room.

If the door is hot or there is heavy smoke in the corridor, stuff wet towels against the base of the door.

Windows are another concern. Hotel windows come in many forms. There are those that can be opened wide (sash windows), those that tilt inward but can only be opened a few inches, sliding windows that lead to a terrace, and sealed windows.

A balcony is a big plus, no matter how small it is and no matter how high up. Take a sheet out on the balcony with you and tie it to the railing. While fire engine ladders cannot reach above the sixth floor, the sheet will alert authorities to where you are. Close the sliding door behind you; if you are nervous about heights, face the wall of the building.

If the window is the kind that opens only a few inches, get a wet towel to put over your head, and kneel at the base of the window, breathing the outside air. It may be uncomfortable and frightening, but you can survive a long time in this situation.

A sash window should not be flung wide open unless you are on a floor low enough to jump out or there is a balcony or fire escape on the other side. First, you need to check the direction of the wind outside. Is it blowing toward you or away from you? If it is blowing toward you, it is safe to open the window wide. But if it is blowing away from you, be careful. With a wide open window, the air can be sucked out of the room, leaving a "vacuum" which the fire and smoke will rush to fill. If the wind is blowing away from you, open the window no more than three inches, and kneel beside it.

The wind direction is even more important in deciding whether or not to break a sealed window. Such windows are made of thick glass and can only be broken by hitting them smack in the middle with a heavy object. The entire window is likely to collapse, creating a very large hole through which the air in your room can be sucked if the wind is blowing away from you. You will be making an irrevocable decision in such a case so don't act if you're not absolutely certain. Unless the wind is blowing toward you, you could be hastening your own demise.

Take care. And begin by making a stink if a hotel seems lax in the matter of fire safety, not only to protect yourself but also the lives of other travelers.

EXPLORERS ANONYMOUS

There are caves and canyons to explore, mountains to climb, rapids to shoot. The natural landscape is beautiful—but it is also dangerous. Accidents can happen, storms can blow up, and if no one knows where you are, there will be no one to come to your rescue. No experienced explorer would think of setting off into the wilderness without making certain that someone in authority knew where he or she was going and how long he or she expected to be gone, yet amateurs and beginners, who are more likely to get in trouble, often just go. Inevitably, some of them are never seen again.

Never set off on any kind of wilderness expedition without registering with a ranger, if you are in a national or state park, or with local police in other wilderness areas.

No explorer should ever be anonymous.

EYE IRRITATIONS

When your eyes are tired, irritated, or you have what feels like a speck in one of them, the wrong thing to do is to rub, which will only cause further irritation. Ophthalmologists recommend blinking the eyes instead.

If there's a foreign particle in your eye, and you can't dislodge it by blinking, gently raise the lid with one hand while looking in a mirror and try to see where it is. If it is on the white of the eye, use a clean tissue to wipe it away. Do not touch it, however, if it is on the cornea; instead, close your eye, and move the eyeball back and forth in order to move the particle onto the white. If that doesn't work, flush your eye with cold water, using an eye cup inverted over the eye socket. (A jigger will also work.) Even after you have removed a particle, there may be some residue irritation because the inside of the lid has been scratched. If the irritation persists, see your physician.

Be careful about using over-the-counter eye drops to "clear up" your eyes. Used occasionally, in moderation, these preparations will do what they claim. But if you use them regularly and often, physicians warn that instead of bringing relief, they can cause chronic irritation.

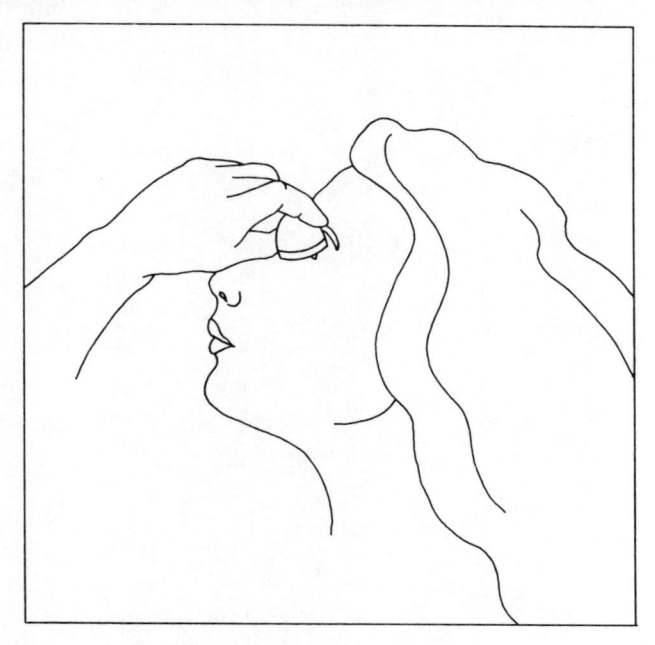

FABRIC STORAGE

You've got an antique quilt, a lace tablecloth, or a silk puff that you want to store away for the summer. You think the best way to keep it safe would be to put it in a large plastic garbage bag. Think again. Textile experts point out that fabrics made of natural fibers need to breathe; otherwise they may mildew. You'll be much better off wrapping your quilt or tablecloth in a cotton sheet.

Make sure the place where you store it has been treated for insects. And never store natural fibers in an attic or basement; they are adversely affected by changes in humidity. Instead, put them in a cool closet.

FAMILY TREES

Family trees are fascinating. Think about the great royal families of Europe, Tudors and Hapsburgs and Romanovs, with all that intermarriage and cross-fertilization going back hundreds of years: it can really put things in perspective. You may be interested in your own family tree. Maybe if you went back far enough, you'd discover that you are, however distantly, descended from someone who came across on the Mayflower, or that even further back, there was some great warrior, inventor, or writer lurking in your bloodlines. Perhaps even royalty.

It could be true. But before you get carried away with the idea, and especially before you pay anyone to research your family tree, there are a few things you should keep in mind. A gentleman who shall remain anonymous reports that as a hobby he traces family trees for people who want to join such organizations as The Sons of The Confederacy. He charges a modest fee to establish that somebody's great-great-grandmother's cousin Luke fought in the Civil War under Robert E. Lee. He admits, however, that problems can arise. Sometimes, he will discover that there is a black branch of the family, for instance. In those cases he simply lops off that branch. Racist? "No doubt," he admits. But the gentleman knows that most people who hire him are paying for a pedigree, not a forgotten family scandal.

Other "researchers" take the opposite tack. You've answered their mail or magazine advertisement, which offers to unearth your family coat of arms. In this case, a "branch" may get tied onto your tree with bailing wire—anything to make a connection with one or another of the thousands of families with historically validated crests.

If you come from a truly prominent family, your family tree will already be well known. If you don't, but are curious, the right way to proceed is to do it yourself, writing letters to every obscure relative yyu can dig up. It will take you a long time, which is why you should always be suspicious of anybody who claims he or she will research the matter for you in a month for only $100. An ersatz family tree can be manufactured in a day by anyone with the right reference books and the information you yourself have provided. Developing a genuine family tree requires a great deal more time than $100 could possibly pay for.

But beware: Many who have traced their family trees find relatives that they wished they never had.

FASTING

"Fasting," wrote the great French philosopher of food, Brillat-Savarin, "is a voluntary abstinence from food with a moral or religious end in view." Fasting to this day plays a role in many religious observances around the world, and the "hunger strike," is often used to make a moral—or at least a political—point. But these days fasting often has an entirely different goal, one which Brillat-Savarin would have been unlikely to approve: to lose weight.

Advocates of fasting, or starvation diets, often claim that not only will you lose weight, but also "cleanse" your body of "toxic" substances. That sounds like a good deal, right? Lose weight and make yourself healthier into the bargain.

Wrong, say a great many physicians and nutritionists. They point out that a lot of the substances that are cleaned out of the body during a fast are actually essential minerals and vitamins. The biochemical changes that take place in your body during a fast can cause sharply lowered blood pressure (with accompanying bouts of dizziness), put an added strain on your liver and kidneys, and, depending on your physical condition, cause a variety of unpleasant and potentially dangerous side effects. Some programs treating obesity have reported considerable success using starvation diets—but the patients were under constant medical supervision, usually in a hospital.

Theodore Berland, author and nutritionist, sums it up in *Rating the Diets*: "Never, never fast on your own for more than a day even for religious or meditative reasons."

If you want to fast longer than that, see your physician.

FEVER REDUCTION

When you have a fever, if you reach for the aspirin or some other fever-reducing compound you may be making a mistake. The idea that fever ought to be controlled developed in the late 1800s, following the commercial introduction of aspirin. But for two thousand years before that, fever was widely believed to be beneficial. It's a concept that goes back as far as Hippocrates, the ancient Greek physician regarded as "the father of medicine." New studies published in several medical journals indicate that the ancients may have been right all along.

Even some pediatricians are now recommending that, when there are no complications, moderate fevers be allowed to run their course. Not only may a moderate fever, even one as high as 103 degrees, shorten the illness, but there is also evidence that fever assists in activating antibiotics and can reduce the chances of other people getting infected.

The studies show that fever acts as an immunological defense against infection. It can even destroy infectious organisms by "burning them out." Tests on infected animals, including such mammals as rabbits and dogs, indicate that the animals whose body temperatures have been allowed to rise are the most likely to survive.

Such experiments have been corroborated by the fact that people who exercise strenuously, including long-distance runners, raise their body temperatures in the process - and appear to be less susceptible to viruses, flus and even the common cold.

FIGHTING DOGS

The best way to stop a dog fight is to spray the dogs with a hose or to dump a bucket of water over them. This is not always possible, of course, but there is one thing you should never do: hit or kick a fighting dog, even your own. The dogs are out of control and they may easily turn on you. Sharp commands may help, or you can try pulling the dogs apart by their tails, but a dog fight often must be allowed to run its course, no matter how frightening that may seem. One dog or the other will often end the fight itself by turning over on its back in a submissive position.

If your dog is on a leash and is attacked by a free-running dog, it is not always wise to try to pull your dog away. You may hinder it from protecting itself. Often the better course is to let go of the leash.

Many localities have laws against free-running dogs. If such is the case in your community, you have every right to request that the owner of a free-running dog that has attacked yours pay for any veterinary expenses. You may not get far with that, especially if the owner shares his dog's belligerence, but it is worth a try.

If your dog is injured, clean any wounds with hydrogen peroxide and then, if necessary, take it to your veterinarian.

FIGURE SKATES

Figure skating has grown enormously in popularity as both a spectator and participatory sport in the United States since the 1960s. Nonetheless, instructors and coaches report that old myths about weak ankles and cold feet are still influencing parents to buy their beginner children skates that don't fit properly. Many people assume that thick socks should be worn under figure skates. They believe that wool socks will help support the child's ankles. And the very word "ice" leads them to conclude the child's feet will freeze without such socks. Both these assumptions are wrong.

First of all, except in unusual cases, there is no such thing as "weak ankles." Children's bones are more flexible than those of adults, but the problem some beginning skaters have in staying erect relates to coordination and balance, not a physical deficiency in the ankles. As to the cold—because figure skates rise over the ankle, they're like little ovens, keeping in the natural warmth of the body. There's more cause to worry about the feet sweating than getting cold.

Amateur and professional figure-skating champions like to have as little cloth between the foot and the leather of the skate as possible and usually wear nothing more than tights. Figure skates should fit like a glove, not a mitten. The closer the fit, the more control the skater has.

You may object that, with a growing child, that's going to mean buying a new pair of skates every year. But if you keep your ears open at any skating rink, you'll find someone anxious to sell a pair of skates a child has outgrown, and you can sell your own child's skates in the same way. Until, of course, your child begins to show promise of being a champion. That's going to mean handmade skates, but if you get that far, you'll know what to do—get a second mortgage.

FIREWORKS

The wrong way to handle fireworks is to handle them at all. Even professionals injure themselves setting off fireworks, and kids playing with small firecrackers blow their fingers off all too often. Follow the advice of your local police and fire department: confiscate any fireworks your child gets his or her hands on and call the parents of any other child who has a supply. Then go see the professional July Fourth display at your local park or waterfront.

FLAMBE FOLLIES

The waiter, or more likely the tuxedoed captain, rolls the cart up to your table. A copper pan is elevated over a low flame. Your *steak au poivre* or your *crepes Suzette* are about to be flamed at tableside. Warmed brandy is dribbled grandly over the food, a long match is lit and touched to the chafing dish. Flames leap; everyone says, "Ahh."

Although it's wonderfully dramatic, this flambe technique is not recommended for home display for two simple reasons: it's not safe and it often doesn't work. When the inexperienced chef pours liquor over the food and then tries to ignite it, as many cookbooks suggest, one of two things is likely to occur: either the flames will sputter wanly for a few seconds and then go out or they'll leap up as though fanned by the devil himself, spattering butter or pan juices and making everyone cringe.

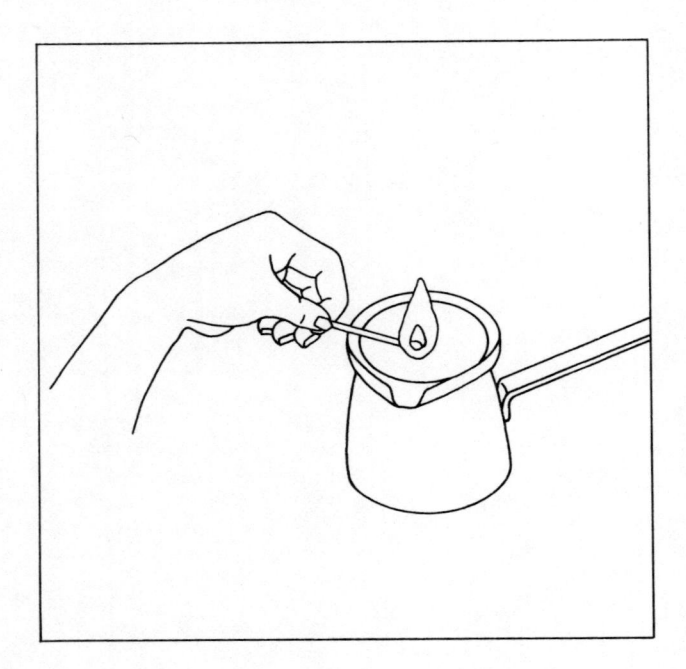

There is a much more successful approach that has the added advantage of being safe. Warm the brandy in a small side pot that has a long handle and a pouring spout. The liquor shouldn't come to a boil, but simply begin to vaporize, sending up an aromatic steam. Then, keeping your body well back from the brandy warmer, light the brandy while it's still in the pot. Once it has begun to flame, pour it over your steak or your dessert. The result will not in all cases be quite as spectacular as it sometimes is in restaurants, but you will achieve a more even flaming and you won't have to rush yourself or anybody else to the hospital.

FLAT TIRE FIRST AID

When it comes to changing a flat tire, many people go wrong before they even leave home. Even if they have a spare in good condition in the trunk, they may not have all the tools necessary to do the job. You need not only a jack for getting the axle off the ground but also a screw driver to help remove the wheel cover and a lug wrench for loosening the lug nuts.

Do you know how your jack operates? There are several different designs. Their operation is fully described in the car manual—but where is that manual, in your glove compartment or back home in a drawer? (When renting a car, always check to see if there is a manual in the car; too often, they are missing.) The manual will also indicate where to place the jack under the car's frame. If you put it in the wrong place, the jack may slip, especially if you haven't parked the car on level terrain.

Serious accidents can occur if a jack does slip and fly out under pressure. Often, along the highway, you will see several people gathered around the person changing the tire. Precisely because jacks *can* slip they shouldn't be there. Get your passengers not only *out of* the car but *away from* the car. (Having them several yards away will also cut down on gratuitous advice). Many people make the mistake of jacking the car too high off the ground. Three inches of clearance beneath the wheel is all you need.

After you have put the spare tire in place, be sure *not* to tighten the lug nuts in order. Move back and forth from top to bottom or side to side to ensure that the wheel is properly balanced.

And remember to replace that spare!

FLOODED CELLARS

If you think your cellar may be flooded don't turn on the lights. Use a flashlight instead. Don't step foot into the water unless you have on rubber boots that rise higher over your legs than the level of the water itself. This is your protection from electrical currents. If you live in an area where flooding occurs with some regularity (even it that's only every few years), have your fuse box and master electrical switches moved from the basement to the top of the cellar stairway or a first- or second-floor closet. That way you can be certain the electricity is off before venturing into possibly dangerous waters.

FOOD POISONING

Suddenly, you have stomach cramps and the beginnings of nausea. Vomiting and diarrhea follow. It could be an intestinal flu, but unless you also have a fever, it is more likely to be food poisoning. Many more people are affected by food poisoning than realize it. That's because the most common form of food poisoning is caused by salmonella bacteria, which have an incubation period of from 12 to 48 hours. Most people think back only to their two previous meals and thus fail to track down the cause of their distress.

Staphylococcal food poisoning, although less common, strikes much more quickly, within a few hours after the contaminated food has been consumed. The physical reaction to staphylococcal food poisoning is similar to that of salmonella poisoning, although it is often even more intense. However, you will probably recover fairly quickly from staphylococcal food poisoning, while the effects of salmonella poisoning can linger for days.

Staphylococcal food poisoning is usually caused by contamination from human or animal waste: that's why there are signs in restaurant restrooms requiring employees to wash their hands. Shellfish from polluted waters are also a danger, which is why oysters, clams, and mussels are subject to careful scrutiny by both state and national agencies. Such watchdog agencies have greatly reduced the incidence of staphylococcal food poisoning. You can further protect yourself and others by reporting to local health authorities any restaurant that shows signs of uncleanliness, from the restrooms to the silverware.

Food poisoning from salmonella bacteria may occur in a restaurant, but the problem often arises from food that is improperly prepared in the home kitchen. Poultry, because of the mass-production techniques used to eviscerate and clean the birds, is particularly susceptible to the spreading of the bacteria; like the one rotten apple that can spoil the barrel, one infected chicken can taint a great many others. (Remember that when you buy chicken parts, they come from many different birds.) Health organizations recommend thoroughly washing whole chickens, ducks and turkeys, or any part, including livers and other innards, in warm water before cooking. Many cookbooks published before the late 1960s either say nothing on the subject of washing poultry or actually advise against it. Julia Child very responsibly reversed herself on this subject once new studies revealed the possible dangers.

After washing your poultry thoroughly, wash your own hands and any surfaces, from cutting board to dishes, on which the poultry has been placed prior to washing. And, above all, *never* stuff a bird until you are ready to pop it in the oven. One of the foremost causes of salmonella poisoning is the holiday turkey that is stuffed the night before cooking. Don't do it. You can prepare the stuffing ahead of time but keep it in a separate container.

FRESH FISH

A family member, friend, next-door neighbor, or you yourself have gone off fishing at the crack of dawn. The adventurers have a good day of it and return in the late afternoon with a plentiful supply of trout, catfish, pike, or mackerel. Fresh fish! Most people assume it's bound to be a lot better than anything you can buy at the fish market. Unfortunately, that isn't necessarily true.

The problem lies in the fact that many amateur anglers are so busy fishing that they don't take the time to eviscerate their catch until just before they start home, or they even wait until they get home. That's a mistake. As such experts as A.J. McClane, for more than 30 years the fishing editor of *Field and Stream*, and Jacqueline Knight, a member of the Fishing Hall of Fame, point out, the digestive process in most fish is extremely potent, and unless the fish is gutted immediately, the digestive enzymes will continue to "eat away" within the intestine for hours after fish is caught, destroying quality, flavor, and hastening spoilage. On most commercial fishing vessels, evisceration takes place immediately, and the fish are promptly placed in ice. Thus, the commercially caught fish that doesn't reach your local market until four days after it was caught will often taste fresher than the fish that was caught eight hours ago but not cleaned at once.

Because, in most cases, it does take so long for commercially caught fish to reach the market, you still need to check for quality and freshness. Here are some of the characteristics to look for:

1. With a whole fish, check the eyes first. They should be clear, bright, and slightly bulging. If they are sunken or milky, don't buy.
2. Press the flesh with your fingers. It should be firm and elastic. If your finger leaves an indentation, the fish has begun to deteriorate.
3. Look at the gills. They should be red. If they've begun to darken, turning brown or gray, turn to another specimen.
4. The skin should be shiny and unblemished.
5. Finally, smell the fish. It should not smell overly fishy but have a clean, clear odor, although some fish, like mackerel, will have a somewhat stronger odor than others.

If you are buying fish filets or steaks that have been precut, look for a firm, moist "clean-cut" appearance, avoiding pieces that show discoloration or dried patches. And use your nose again.

FROSTBITE REMEDIES

The old-fashioned remedy for frostbite is to rub the frostbitten extremities with snow. Don't, physicians warn. While it is true that a *blanket* of snow can sometimes afford protection against bitter temperatures brought even lower by the windchill factor, frostbitten hands or feet are *already* damaged and thus it's too late for such protection. In addition, a rubbing action may cause the skin to break, compounding the problem.

On the other hand, you shouldn't opt for warm or hot water either, which has the effect of cooking the damaged cells. Instead, begin with cool water, in order to gradually bring the flesh to room temperature. If you thaw frozen fingers or toes too fast, the tissues will begin to break down. Take it slowly; as pinkness begins to return to the affected parts, slightly warmer water can be used. But never hot.

FUNERAL COSTS

The funeral home business has never been the same since the publication of Jessica Mitford's *The American Way of Death*. Since then, there have been many newspaper and magazine articles, as well as local and national television investigative reports on the psychological wiles used by some funeral directors to persuade the mourning family members to purchase the most expensive coffin and agree to the most elaborate funeral arrangements for the departed. While there are many highly reputable funeral homes that do not indulge in such manipulation, you can't be too careful.

It's very simple. The choice of coffin and funeral arrangements should not be made by the person most affected but by some other family member who, however sorrowful, is less likely to be talked into spending more than is required or appropriate because of grief or even guilt. If you have no close relatives and must make such choices yourself, take along someone you trust who is less affected, a friend, your lawyer, anyone who can lay a hand on your arm and say, "Don't you think something simpler would be more appropriate?"

Don't compound your grief by saddling yourself with funeral expenses that you will have difficulty paying for.

FURNITURE SANDING

There it was, the perfect table. You found it in a secondhand furniture store or picked it up at a country auction. It's the right size, of pleasing design and is solidly put together. Of course, it is kind of beat-up and will obviously need to be refinished. But that shouldn't take much time, no more than a weekend. You can sand down the rough spots and once you put on a couple of coats of good varnish or paint, it will look just fine.

Oh no, it won't. It may look passable, but that's about it. Refinishing furniture, according to the experts, is a time-consuming and painstaking job—although professionals insist that it can also be satisfying and rewarding.

The crucial step in refinishing furniture is the sanding down to raw wood of *all* surfaces. The most common mistake made by amateurs, according to H. W. Kuhn, author of *Refinishing Furniture* and a professional refinisher himself, is to assume that the varnish or paint will hide any underlying sins. It won't.

All the experts agree that to get a really good finish, it is necessary to sand the piece of furniture at least three times, with three different grades of sandpaper. Begin with a medium-coarse grade, then go over it again with a medium-fine paper, and finally, use a fine-grade polishing paper. Since various experts recommend different brands of sandpaper (and because the code numbers for those papers can vary from brand to brand), it's best to consult your local hardware store. Tell the proprietor what you're doing, and ask for his or her advice.

Can you use an electric sander? Yes, as a first step, if the furniture has a heavy coat of paint or deep scratches. But even with electric sanding, you should still use three grades of paper to complete the job by hand.

When you are sanding, you should always go with the grain of the wood. The natural inclination is to move your arm in an arc, which cuts across the grain. Instead, move your arm back and forth in a straight line, as though you were ironing a pair of pants. When it comes to rounded surfaces or moldings, Frederic Taubes, author of *Antique Finishing for Beginners*, recommends wrapping the sandpaper around dowels of the appropriate thickness.

GARAGE SALES

Garage sales, the personal flea market, are a singularly American institution. But, like the flea markets of Europe, or marketplaces in general in the Mideast and the Orient, they should offer the opportunity for bargaining.

As you clean out your attic, cellar, or closets, choosing the items you want to sell, do not, old hands at this game recommend, make out tags with specific prices. Instead, think about how much you'd like to get for the item and make a mental note of it.

At the actual sale, wait for your customers to approach you about the price of a given piece. If they've picked it out, it means they want it. Then, in the ancient tradition of the marketplace, quote them a price that is a little more than you would actually expect to get. The customer then has the opportunity to make a counteroffer. If the counteroffer is ridiculously low, simply say that you can't sell the object for that price, and the person may come back up some. If you are prepared to spend a little time bargaining back and forth, you can often get pretty much what you wanted in the first place.

GARLIC ODOR

Garlic, that most pungent member of the onion family, has always been a source of controversy. While the Egyptians worshiped it, the ancient Greeks despised it to the degree that they forced criminals to eat it as a way of purifying themselves of their crimes. The irascible eighteenth-century Scottish novelist Tobias Smollett stated that he had been almost poisoned with garlic during his travels in France and Italy. Percy Bysshe Shelley, on his first visit to Italy, wrote to a friend in England: "What do you think? Young women of rank actually eat—you will never guess what—*garlick*! Our poor friend Lord Byron is quite corrupted by living among these people."

Garlic advocates—among them explorers, athletes, and physicians—have extolled its health-giving properties down through the centuries. Dr. Norton F. Brown, former administrator at Roosevelt Hospital, used to say that there was nothing better you could put into your body than garlic. Food authority James Beard has said that he can never have enough of the flavor of fresh garlic. Chef Louis Diat put it unequivocally: "Garlic is the Fifth Element. As important to our existence as earth, air, fire and water. Without garlic I simply would not care to live."

But even if you love garlic, the problem of the odor does arise. You cannot wash the smell from your hands with soap and water. No amount of toothbrushing or gargling with mouth washes will eradicate garlic breath.

The right way to counteract the odor of garlic is with lemon and parsley, two foods whose flavors are often combined with the pungent bulb in recipes because they marry well with it. To remove the smell of garlic from your hands after chopping it (and it should always be chopped; crushing it in a press tends to make it bitter), take a half lemon and squeeze the juice over your dry hands. Rub your hands together vigorously, and then rinse them under cold water. To sweeten your breath after eating garlic, chew and swallow a sprig or two of fresh parsley, preferably the more intensely flavored curly parsley. Then you can go out into the world without having garlic haters recoil from you in horror.

GAS LEAKS

What do you do if you smell gas—not a faint odor seeping out of an extinguished pilot light, but a strong, pervasive odor of leaking gas? Is it coming from the street? Is it leaking from the basement of the building you are in, whether home, apartment building, or commercial structure? You'd better investigate, right?

Wrong.

Don't spend any time investigating on your own. A gas leak can turn into an explosion in seconds with the ignition of a single spark.

Utility companies regularly send out pamphlets telling you what to do if you believe there's a gas leak, whether in a building or in the gas main outside. But you don't really need the pamphlet. As a representative of Consolidated Edison of New York City succinctly put it, "Call your utility company and get out of there."

Yes, warn others in the building, or immediate neighbors if the leak is coming from a main. But don't take the time to argue. Tell them to get out, fast, and do the same yourself.

GLASS DOOR WARNINGS

You have an old screened-in porch, or a "Florida room" that's half wall and half window. It looks tacky and old-fashioned, and you have a few extra dollars, so you have it all reconstructed. Now there's a sheer glass wall with sliding doors leading out onto the patio. It looks so sleek and clean you'd hardly know it's there.

Wherein lies the danger.

Every year thousands of people, especially in the Sun Belt states, have serious home accidents because they think a glass door is open when it's closed. The lucky ones are merely knocked out cold or break a nose. The unlucky ones walk or run right through the glass. It happens to kids running out to the pool, to nearsighted visiting relatives, and to the guy next door who gets a little tipsy at your barbecue.

Almost all these accidents occur when the person is moving from the shadowed interior of the house toward the bright outdoors. When the light is right—or, rather, wrong—the closed glass door looks as though it is open.

So, if you're thinking of putting in a glass wall leading to your patio, swimming pool, or garden, do it right and install a door that's made of tinted glass, to distinguish it from the rest of the window-wall. If you've already got a window-wall, buy some colored tape and make a design on the door so that people know it's there. That may not be classy, but it can prevent dangerous accidents.

A window is to *see* through. A door is to *walk* through. And they ought to be clearly differentiated.

GOSSIP GUIDELINES

Gossip can serve a useful purpose: it is one of the ways in which we order society and an expression of human curiosity. We can learn about ourselves from gossip and how we feel about the world. In small towns, gossip is both a form of social intercourse and a way of livening things up. Life is unimaginable in Washington, D.C. without gossip and rumor, and they are equally important to the social status of the party-going regulars of major cities.

But gossip has its darker side as well. Even in "innocent" gossip, someone is almost always being maligned, even if indirectly. You may talk about how much you pity a woman whose husband is unfaithful; but in so doing you are broadcasting information (or speculation) about the couple's intimate life and also expressing your poor opinion of the husband in question. There is always, in any exchange of gossip, someone who is being targeted for retribution.

We are all prone to gossip; but sooner or later all of us are also victims of it. That's something we should remember next time we are tempted to pass on the latest dirt.

There is one cardinal rule to keep in mind when it comes to gossip: never tell anyone the nasty things somebody else is saying about them, their spouse, or close relatives. The person may know already that a mate is cheating, for example, or may not want to know. Gossiping behind people's backs is destructive enough. Confronting a person with the "truth" about a loved one is far worse. Ask yourself, "What am I getting out of this?" and think twice before opening your mouth.

GRASS GROWING

Look out your window at that lawn. Do you have bare spots, yellow patches, weeds galore, depressions where water gathers after a rainfall? You're doing something—maybe several things—wrong. Here are ten mistakes you may be making.

1. You haven't turned over the soil to a deep enough level before seeding your lawn. Six inches is the minimum.
2. You haven't used the proper combination of grass seeds for the area of the country you live in or for the soil and light conditions on your property. "Merion" Kentucky bluegrass, common bluegrass, red fescue, and ryegrass are the most common seeds used, but their proportion in a mixture should vary according to conditions. Ask for advice at your local garden center.
3. You've seeeed your lawn at the wrong time of year. Early fall is best, mid to late spring second best; never sow a lawn in the heat of summer.
4. You are trying to grow grass in an area that doesn't receive enough sunlight. Even so-called shade grasses need a minimum of six hours of sunlight a day. Otherwise you're better off with a groundcover such as pachysandra or some form of paving.
5. You haven't rolled the soil enough, resulting in a settling of the ground that allows water to collect.
6. You've been manic about rolling your lawn, compacting the soil to a hardness that inhibits root establishment.
7. You haven't fertilized your lawn sufficiently.
8. You've neglected applying weed-killers.
9. You haven't watered your lawn enough.
10. Face it, when it comes to the lawn, you're lazy.

GUESTS ON THE HOUR

It is hard to say which is more annoying: guests who always arrive early, and catch you still getting dressed or with sticky hands in the kitchen, or those who are invariably late and throw the whole rhythm of your planning off. But there is no use getting angry: these people simply can't help themselves.

Experts on etiquette, however, recommend certain counter-measures you can take. Early birds should always be invited to arrive 15 minutes to half an hour later than you want to see them, depending on how much they usually jump the gun. The tardy souls should be invited for at least half an hour earlier than any other guests. Of course, once in a great while, the late ones will make a superhuman effort to get there at the time you've designated, so you'd better be ready for them, just in case. Smile sweetly and tell them you invited them a little early so you'd have a chance to talk before the mob arrived.

Always remember that a few well-chosen, unhurtful lies are an essential part of any host's repertoire. That also goes for being a guest, for that matter.

GUMMING IT UP

The most prevalent noncontagious disease in the United States is peridontal disease. At least 80 percent of the population suffers from gum problems at some point in life. With the advent of fluoridation of public water supplies and the proliferation of fluoridated toothpastes, actual tooth decay has become a secondary dental concern. It's not tooth decay but receding gums and diseased root canals that dentists now focus on.

The villain is dental plaque, which builds up at an astonishing rate. It begins to form between the teeth within hours of a thorough cleaning at a dentist's office. If it isn't removed by flossing—no amount of brushing will get rid of it—it hardens and forms tartar.

If your gums are bleeding, you have gum disease, and you need to get the tartar removed. (There is one exception—pregnant women sometimes suffer from bleeding gums because of hormonal changes that have nothing to do with dental care.) Once your teeth are free from tartar, dentists advise (no, change that to insist) you *must* floss if you want to avoid future problems, possibly extremely expensive ones.

GUNS IN THE CLOSET

The liquor store owner in a big city may indeed need to carry a licensed, loaded gun to protect himself from robbery.

The rural family may indeed want to have a collection of rifles for use in the hunting season.

But *loaded* guns in the home are a different matter. You can tell yourself that they are a protection against burglars. Even Nancy Reagan has admitted that during the years when she and her husband were private citizens, she kept a "tiny little gun" by her bedside for protection when Ronald was traveling. There is a problem, however. While statistics vary from year to year and from one part of the country to another, in an overwhelming majority of cases, loaded guns that are kept in the home end up being used against a relative, neighbor, or friend in a moment of fury, as suicide weapons, or as the instruments of tragic accidents.

Law enforcement officials beg you: keep your guns and ammunition in a locked closet or other place where they cannot be gotten at too easily. Even a few moments of reflection can save someone's life.

HANG GLIDING TAKE-OFFS

Hang gliding appeals to man's most romantic and ancient dreams of being able to fly. And it looks so easy.

Well, it's not.

Hang gliding experts advise the novice to start very small indeed, taking off from a hillock no more than ten feet high. At most you will be in the air for a little more than two seconds. But you also won't injure yourself if you come crashing to the ground. Only slowly, as you develop the "hang" of the sport, should you move to higher and higher positions from which to take off.

It's a time-consuming learning process, but a necessary one for safety reasons. And the experts warn, never bow to peer pressure to take off from higher ground than you are sure you are ready for. Hang gliding is a "macho" sport, and you are likely to be pressured to take risks. Don't.

HANGOVER CURES

Of course, it shouldn't have happened in the first place, but that's not the point: you feel *awful*. Your head is buzzing, your tongue feels as though it were covered with library paste, and your stomach is asking serious questions about what you've done to it.

How can you "cure" that hangover?

The oldest of remedies is "hair of the dog": a shot of whatever you were drinking the night before. There are two problems with this remedy, however. First, if your stomach is queasy, a shot of liquor may cause you to throw up. Second, you've already poisoned your system enough; adding to it hardly seems sensible.

Another well-known remedy is to down a prairie oyster. This concoction of an unbroken egg yolk, Worcestershire sauce, and hot pepper sauce, to be swallowed at one gulp without breaking the yolk, is most indelibly associated with Christopher Isherwood's Sally Bowles, heroine of *I Am a Camera* and *Cabaret*. The great food writer M.F.K. Fisher is a strong advocate of prairie oysters, which she consumes not only for hangovers but also as a pick-me-up before facing such unpleasant duties as going to the dentist. She adds an ounce of cognac to her prairie oysters, as does John Doxat, author of *The World of Drinks and Drinking*. We are dealing with hair of the dog again here, but at least the egg yolk provides protein as well. This cure is obviously not for the squeamish or the cholesterol-conscious.

The Italians swear by *Fernet Branca*, medicinal bitters that contain 39 percent alcohol along with everything else, from aloes to myrrh to saffron. Regarded as being good for the liver and soothing to the stomach, *Fernet Branca* has a flavor that is, to say the least, controversial. Some people like the taste so much they drink it as an aperitif; others can't abide the stuff.

The French espouse what is probably the healthiest of hangover cures: onion soup. The broth is easy to get down, and nutritious, and many physicians acknowledge the mysterious medicinal powers of the onion family. The soup is often eaten *before* going to bed, however, as a preventive rather than a cure. Another preventive favored by many is warm milk before retiring. It not only coats the stomach, but also impedes the absorption of alcohol into the bloodstream (even better if taken *prior to* the drinks). Others drink several glasses of water before turning in for the night, which serves to rehydrate the system.

Finally, there are vitamins. Because alcohol depletes the system of both vitamins C and B, many people tout the efficacy of taking these vitamins either the night before or the morning after.

But, whatever the cure or preventive, there is no doubt that a good night's sleep is as important as anything else.

HEART ATTACK SYMPTOMS

Although the mortality rate for heart disease has declined more than 20 percent since the late 1960s, due to advances in treatment and a greater emphasis on preventive medicine, approximately 650,000 Americans die each year from heart attacks. According to the American Heart Association, many of these deaths could have been prevented if the heart attack victims were treated more quickly. The problem is that so many people ignore heart attack symptoms, waiting hours before seeking medical help. And by then it is often too late.

People persuade themselves that the pain or pressure they are experiencing in the chest is merely indigestion; even if pain is also present in the left arm or both arms, people pass it off as "arthritis," or blame it on too much exercise. Don't be foolish. If you have pain *or* pressure in the chest that lasts for more than fifteen minutes, seek medical assistance immediately. The lower jaw, neck, back, or upper abdomen may also be affected by pain. Breathing difficulties, heavy sweating, and nausea are other symptoms that may or may not be present.

Don't tell yourself, "This will pass." What passes may be your life.

HEAT REACTIONS

People often use the word sunstroke to describe a wide range of heat reactions, from mild to life threatening. A distinction, however, should be made between heat exhaustion and heatstroke. Either can be brought on suddenly by exposure to unaccustomed high temperatures, especially when combined with physical effort. Dizziness, nausea, profuse perspiring, and some elevation of the temperature are the signs of heat exhaustion. Heat exhaustion is treated by rest in a cool place and the replacement of lost fluids and salt.

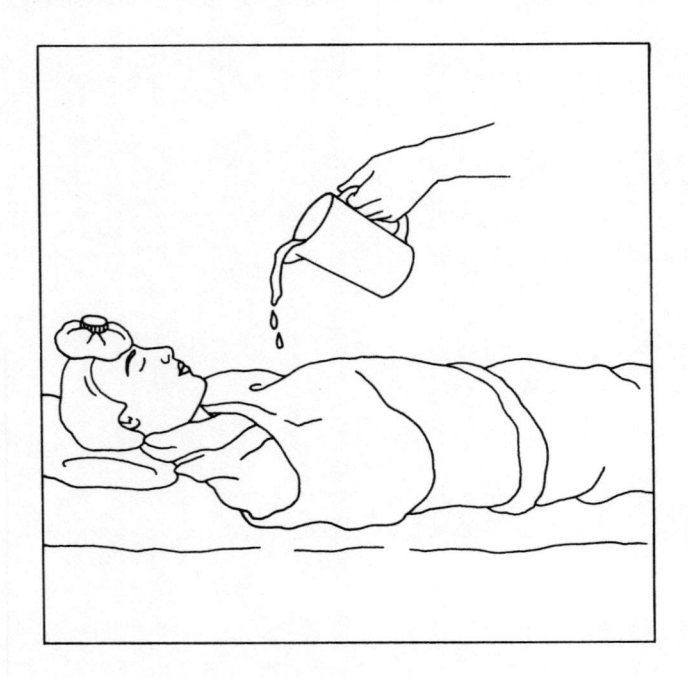

Heatstroke is far more serious. Visual disturbances and nausea are present, but because the brain's ability to control the body's heat regulation is overwhelmed, perspiration does not occur. As a result, very high internal temperatures are reached, and the skin becomes hot and dry. In extreme cases, unconsciousness occurs. Heatstroke demands prompt treatment. The victim's body may be wrapped in a sheet, with cool water poured over it repeatedly. An ice pack should be placed on the head. Immersion in cool or tepid water can also help, but the water should not be ice cold, or it may cause further shock to the system. If the victim is unconscious, medical treatment, including the use of stimulants, is urgently needed.

If you have suffered from even mild heat exhaustion, do not try to resume regular activities too soon. It can easily be two or more days before exertion is advisable. If you suffer heat exaustion or heatstroke once, you should be very careful in the future. Heatstroke victims, in particular, become more liable to future episodes and should make special efforts to shield the head and the back of the neck from the sun.

HICCUP-UPS

According to the *Guinness Book of World Records*, a certain Charles Osborne of Anthen, Iowa, has been hiccuping without cease since 1922. That's more than 60 years of hiccups, but despite his affliction, he has been married twice and fathered eight children. Hiccups can be physically debilitating, however. During his final illness, Pope Pius XII developed a severe case of hiccups which, because of his weakened state, were believed to have hastened his death.

Physicians do not know how to cure hiccups. That's because they don't really know what causes them. There are a number of theories, but none of them has ever led to a definitive cure.

We do have, however, a raft of folk remedies available:

Hold your breath.
Drink a glass of water out of the wrong side.
Swallow a tablespoon of sugar without water.
Have a friend scream unexpectedly in your ear.
Stand on your head.

All of these remedies have proved effective, some of the time. Unfortunately, they do not work consistently, even for the same person. Some people find that taking an antacid can help, which is as close as we have come to "medical" reasoning.

More alluringly, there are those who claim to have had their hiccups cured when they received a sudden passionate kiss, of the French variety, which literally took their breath away. This may not be the "right" way to cure hiccups, but there certainly seems nothing wrong with trying it.

HOUSEPLANT WATERING

Do you religiously water your plants twice a week? Do you give plants in clay pots the same amount of water as those in plastic pots? Do you give your plants the same amount of water year-round?

No wonder they're dying.

Different plants, according to horticultural experts, require varying amounts of water, depending upon their *genus*, the potting medium, the humidity in the air, and other factors.

Plants of thin-leaved varieties need more water than those with hairy or waxy leaves. Thus a fern needs more water than an African violet, a spathiphyllum more than a succulent such as the popular "lawyer's tongue."

Because the porous clay pot absorbs water from the soil and "sweats" it away into the atmosphere, plants in clay pots need to be watered more frequently than those in nonporous plastic pots. The humidity in the air is also important. In winter, the dry air created by central heating will make it necessary to water plants more often. Some houseplants require more water during their period of bloom.

But the ultimate test is made with the fingers. Is the soil at the top of the pot drying out? It's time to water. If it is moist, wait a day or two and check again. And never let a plant sit in water for more than an hour. If water remains in the saucer, or other container, pour it off. Because every variety of plant requires a different amount of water, the testing of the soil with the fingers remains the best all-around guide.

HOUSE SEATS FOR SALE

A new show has opened on Broadway, a touring production is coming to your city, or your stagestruck child is performing in summer theater in Pennsylvania, Ohio, Florida, or Texas. You know someone connected with the theater, the publicity firm involved, or a member of the cast or crew. Maybe, you think, you can get "house seats." Well, maybe you can, but if you think they are going to be free, think again.

Every theater does indeed retain a certain number of house seats until the last minute, the number varying according to the seating capacity. If you know the right person, you may be able to get hold of a couple of house seats. They will be the best and the most expensive seats in the theater. But, unless you are a very important person indeed—a major star the producer is courting for his or her next production, a movie producer interested in the film rights—you probably won't get a house seat for nothing. A discount, maybe, free, unlikely. If you're a spouse or lover of someone in the show, you might get a free ticket provided the house isn't sold out, but if you want to be sure of a seat, you'd better buy it. It's a matter of the profit margin, which is usually very slim in the theater.

The only people who regularly get free seats to the theater are critics—and they get two tickets once, when the show opens. If a critic wants to see a show again, whether for his own pleasure, or to check out how it's holding up after a year's run, he'll have to pay like anyone else.

It is true that if you know the right people, you can sometimes get free tickets to a flop. This is called "papering the house," and the free tickets are given out because a few extra bodies sitting around, and hopefully laughing or applauding because they know someone onstage, helps to give the paying customers the notion that they aren't seeing a disaster after all.

Otherwise, though, house seats are very much a pay-as-you-go proposition.

IMPRESSING THE BOSS

It's a classic situation. You've been on your new job for four months and everything seems to be going very well. Time to invite your immediate boss and his wife (or her husband, as the case may be) to dinner. You and your spouse contrive a splendid spread, caviar with cocktails, prime rib or a poached bass for a main course, fine wines, elegant table settings.

Your boss's reaction may be any one of the following:

"These people have real class. I'm impressed."

"These people are living beyond their means. Is he/she looking for my job?"

"I hate gourmet food."

Or, take another sittation. You come in early every morning, and leave late every evening. Your boss's reactions can cover a considerable range:

"This one's a real go-getter. I like that."

"He/she is awfully ambitious. I bet we lose him/her to another firm before you can blink."

"I wonder if he/she has problems at home?"

The point here is don't make assumptions about what is going to impress your boss. You may end up undermining yourself. Find out for sure. Ask other members of the firm, discreetly, what the boss likes and dislikes. Keep your eyes and ears open. Pick up on signals. Does your boss have a sandwich at his or her desk for lunch? Watch that gourmet treatment. Does your boss have family pictures all over the office? If so, your long hours may be taken as a sign that you're neglecting your own family.

If you want to impress your boss, discover who he or she really is as a person, what he or she values in life. But, most important, be yourself. Nothing makes a worse impression than phoniness. Above all, avoid trying to impress, not your boss, but yourself.

INSOMNIA

It's two o'clock in the morning and you still haven't fallen asleep. Or, even more common, you keep waking up again and again during the night. What do you do? Some people get up and have another alcoholic drink. Many reach for the pill bottle. Neither approach is a wise one, according to Samuel Dunkell, M.D., head of the Sleep Disorder Clinic at New York Hospital and author of *Sleep Positions* (Morrow, 1977).

Small doses of alcohol do have a sedative effect, but heavy use of alcohol results in suppression of the important REM (Rapid Eye Movement) phases during which we dream; REM phase suppression causes sleep fragmentation. Sleeping pills, both prescription and nonprescription, are enormously overused. Nonprescription pills quickly lose their effectiveness as tolerance builds up, and psychological dependence on them can lead to chronic insomnia. There are drawbacks to prescription pills as well. Some newer drugs do not cause the physical addiction of barbiturates, but they often result in dependency and mask the real problem, which is usually psychological.

What should you do? One answer for temporary insomnia lies in the recent discovery that L-tryptophan, a chemical that aids sleep, is found in protein-rich foods such as dairy products and meats. Drinking a glass of milk, preferably warm, will help you as much as, if not more than, any over-the-counter pill. Turkey, the best source of L-tryptophan, would be the ideal food to eat shortly before bedtime. (This may be why we feel so sleepy after Thanksgiving dinner.)

For chronic insomnia, consult your physician, but be sure to explore possible psychological causes.

JANGLY JEWELRY AND OTHER AUDIENCE DISTURBANCES

Audiences at public entertainment of every kind get ruder every day. The woman in front of you at the ballet is wearing at least six bracelets on each arm. It is overly warm in the theater, and she picks up her program and begins to fan herself. Jangle, jangle, jangle, and not in tune with Tchaikovsky, either. Or the loudmouth behind you at the theater keeps trying to impress his date by loudly whispering footnotes to the drama on stage. At the movies, there's the older couple who take turns repeating all the funny lines to one another, which means that you (and they) miss the next joke, at which point they ask one another, "What was that?" And these are all adults, not the teenage marauders who are the scourge of the film industry as well as their local theater.

Some blame it all on television. Everybody has gotten used to blathering away at home and forgets that a public theater is not a living room. But television can't really account for the extent of the problem. There have always been inconsiderate people who consistently fail to respect the rights of others. But there's no denying that their breed increases apace.

The way to handle these people is to politely ask them to desist. Right? Nonsense.

Such people are thoughtless, selfish, and rude to begin with. If you try tt deal with them politely, they will take offense anyway, or else assume that your very politeness means that you can safely be ignored. What you must do is to nail them, and nail them good. Herewith a few statements I have heard people make in such circumstances over the years that have proved 100 percent effective.

To the lady with the bracelets, during a scene break: "Madame, if you are auditioning for the timpani section of the orchestra, may I suggest you go around to the stage door."

To the ever-knowledgeable loudmouth, at intermission, spoken so that everyone around you can hear: "Excuse me, Sir, but I wonder if you could speak a little louder during the next act. I couldn't really catch all your comments."

To the couple who repeat all the jokes: "You know, if you'd listen instead of talking, we might all find out what the actors are saying."

Dealing with uproarious teenagers is another matter. Your reprimands will probably be ignored, and verbal abuse can quickly degenerate into violence. The best and safest bet is to get an usher, preferably brawny. Often, however, it's simply less emotionally draining to move to another seat if you possibly can.

JIGSAW PUZZLEMENT

The most common mistake that people make when trying to put together a jigsaw puzzle, according to Mary and James Gilleran, long-time aficionados of these visual teasers, is to begin at the center of the picture. The center may seem like a logical starting place, since it generally features the strongest pictorial element. But this approach invariably proves to be more time-consuming.

Begin by piecing together the "frame," the Gillerans advise. This is easy to do, since all the pieces will have one straight (or in the case of circular puzzles, perfectly curved) line.

The remainder of the pieces should be divided into separate piles according to their color. Some of these piles may subsequently need subdividing according to paler and darker tones, especially if you are dealing with a picture that has expanses of sky or grass. At all times keep the illustration of the puzzle propped up in front of you so that you can refer to it with ease. Work from the frame toward the center from each corner of the puzzle. If you get stuck, move to a different area.

The beauty of this system, the Gillerans note, is that as you approach the end of your task the center portion will fall rapidly into place, increasing your sense of accomplishment. There is nothing more frustrating, they feel, than struggling to get the central figures fleshed out and then concluding the jigsaw with a tedious fitting together of anonymous pieces of the background.

JOGGING SHOES

Jogging is supposed to be good for your health. It tunes up your cardiovascular system, exercises both upper and lower body muscles, and helps you lose weight, or at least keep it down. The jogging craze, however, has also jammed the waiting rooms of podiatrists across the nation, as joggers hobble in to have the pains in their feet and legs diagnosed. The most frequent ailments are inflammation of knee cartilage, shin splints, stretched or swollen Achilles tendons, bone spurs on the heel, and stress fractures of the small bones of the feet.

The problem is that when you jog, your feet hit the ground with a force two to four times your body weight; over the course of a mile that happens 1,600 times. That's a lot of pedal punishment. According to the experts, however, many of the problems joggers develop in their feet and legs could be alleviated, if people would stop jogging in inappropriate or ill-fitting shoes.

Ordinary sneakers or tennis shoes are out; they won't cushion your feet sufficiently, nor do they supply sufficient arch support. You need shoes specifically designed for jogging, and, if you're serious about the sport, expensive ones. Spending an extra $15 or $20 for really well-made jogging shoes can save you hundreds of dollars in medical fees. Don't be pennywise and pound foolish.

In addition, the shoes need to fit properly for running, not walking. A jogging shoe should hug your heel firmly, but not too tightly, and there should be extra room in the toes. Because of the extra pressure on your feet when you jog, they need more room to move within the shoes than when you are walking. So forget fashion, bargain prices, and brand-name chic, and look for the right shoe for you.

JOHNNY CAN READ

Your child is having trouble reading? Very likely *you* have contributed to the problem, unless your child has a special physical or psychological handicap. Study after study, whether carried out by government agencies, private research groups, or teaching universities, shows that parents who enjoy and make a habit of reading themselves, and who make a practice of reading to their children before the youngsters are able to read for themselves, have enormous impact on the reading ability of the child. Stop blaming television (good readers watch television as well as bad readers), and stop blaming the schools (teachers can't inspire a child who goes home to a family with no interest in reading). If you want your child to be a good reader, *you* have got to start the ball rolling by reading aloud to the child from the time he or she is able to comprehend simple language and by encouraging the child to read books on his or her own subsequently. *Nothing* can take the place of your example and your encouragement.

KEYHOLE KIDS

One of the most frequent complaints that sex therapists, family advisers, and advice columnists receive is this: "Now that we have kids running around, our sex life has gone to pot."

Children necessarily cause a reordering of priorities, time allotment, and feelings. But therapists always get suspicious when the presence of children is put forward as the *cause* of diminishing sexual activity between the parents. Several questions immediately arise. Is one or both of the parents using the presence of children to avoid sexual contact that they had problemsswith in the first place? Is the suddenly abstinent husband punishing the wife for paying so much attention to the child? Does the wife fear having more children? What's really going on? There may be many different answers, and the working out of such problems can be complex and time-consuming.

But one thing, therapists agree, is certain. Parents who want to continue a rich and affectionate sex life can do so. They have to want to make the time to be alone, they have to teach their children that there are times that belong to them alone, and they have to ensure that they can have that time without being interrupted.

Ensuring that time alone begins with one simple, practical step, which therapists find themselves suggesting over and over again.

Put a lock on your bedroom door.

KISSY KISSY

First there is the social kiss.

In America, it is usually planted on the left cheek, although left-handers, as in everything else, may head in the opposite direction. In much of Europe, both cheeks are kissed, starting with the left and moving to the right. In America, if a man and a woman know one another well, a quick peck with mutually pursed lips is acceptable. In Italy, men think nothing of kissing one another; in America, the very idea gives most men the willies.

The romantic kiss is something else. Those who kiss with their mouths closed are disdained. What the Americans and English call the French kiss, with the mouth open and tongues intertwined, the French call *le baiser l'anglaise*, or the English kiss. No one, it seems, wishes to take responsibility for this delightfully unsanitary mingling. The Eskimos rub noses instead.

The social kiss raises problems, the main one being: how long do you have to know someone and how well before a kiss is exchanged? Experts on etiquette tend to disagree on these issues but skirt them by suggesting that the woman may indicate that a kiss is welcome by lifting her head slightly and turning her cheek to the man. It is rude not to respond. If you happen to be in show business, you can start kissing almost immediately. It's usually okay to kiss on a second meeting. If you've heard a great deal about someone from a mutual friend, and the friend is present, you can even kiss that someone on the first meeting. Even men in show business are unembarrassed about kissing one another. Johnny Carson is on record as finding all this show-business kissy-kissy stuff a bit much, but he has no escape. He stands trapped behind that "Tonight Show" desk, and even actresses or singers he has never met before rush up and kiss him. Perhaps that is because he has already been in their bedrooms for one thousand and one nights; they feel as though they know him.

And then there is hand kissing. In Europe, when a man kisses a woman's hand, it can be a sign of respect, of flirtation, or a cover-up for adultery. Whatever the case, the woman's hand should be lifted to just below the level of the man's chin, upon which he inclines his head to meet it. The meaning of the kiss is conveyed with the eyes. Indeed, when deciding in any situation to kiss or not to kiss, the eyes offer the best evidence of how to proceed.

KNIVES AT THE READY

Do very sharp knives make you nervous? Are you afraid of cutting yourself? The fact is that knives with dull cutting edges are more dangerous than sharp knives. A dull knife is much more likely to slip or skitter when you are using it.

Aside from being safer, sharp knives are essential to good cooking. First-rate knives are expensive but worth the investment: a superior knife will last for 10 to 20 years. That is, if proper care is taken. Proper care means sharpening a knife after each use. It only takes a few seconds to bring a knife back to ideal sharpness, so keep a sharpener in your knife rack or hanging next to it, and give your knives a quick honing on a regular basis. It is much more difficult—and more time-consuming—to "bring back" a knife that has been allowed to become dull.

Never wash a good knife in a dishwasher. The heat will not only hasten the disintegration of the wooden handle, but will adversely affect the molecular structure of the steel—which was originally forged by heat. Wash your knives in hot soapy water and dry them immediately. Then run them over the sharpening tool and put them away, ready to do your culinary bidding the next time.

LAMB CARVING

Manny and Louis, brothers and butchers by trade, like their father before them, own the Court Square Meats Shop in Long Island City, New York (in the borough of Queens, right across the East River from midtown Manhattan). Manny and Louis supply a number of Queens restaurants, as well as their ethnically mixed and economically iverse neighborhood. They also pride themselves on their expertise, in both cooking and carving quality meats, and they'll gladly share it with anyone who's interested.

According to Louis, the most common mistake people make is carving meat against the grain instead of with it. That's particularly true with a leg of lamb. Many people overcook lamb to begin with, instead of serving it pink in the French fashion, but then they compound the error by turning it on its side and cutting it into hunks against the grain.

How do you do it right?

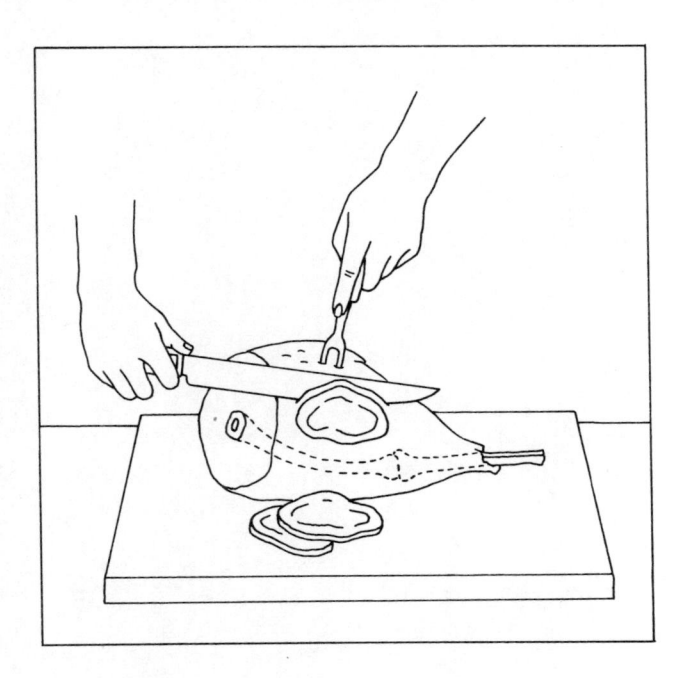

You put the cooked leg of lamb on a platter or cutting block with the bone side down. During cooking, the meat will have drawn back from the shank, which should be pointed to the left of the person carving if he or she is right-handed, or to the right if he or she is left-handed. The knife you use is important. Lamb is most easily carved with a fairly long and flexible knife. Start about a third of the way down, cutting toward the shank end. Once you've removed the top slices, turn the leg on its side and make long, narrow slices from the remaining meat.

LAXATIVE USAGE

Which of the following statements are true and which are false?

1. The normal range of bowel movements is between three times a day and three times a week.
2. Stress, traveling, and dietary changes are major causes of temporary constipation.
3. Over-the-counter laxatives work to relieve constipation in very different ways.
4. The regular use of stimulant laxatives is a major cause of constipation.

True or false? All are true.

Health authorities across the board agree that laxatives are one of the most overused and misused of pharmaceutical products. Both the misuse and the overuse of laxatives are based on the myth that a healthy person is supposed to have one bowel movement a day. In fact, we all have different bodily rhythms, responsive to a multitude of factors, and the person who has three bowel movements a day is no less and no more "regular" than the person who has three a week. Stress, traveling, dietary changes, or other factors may cause the rhythm to change, either increasing or decreasing the number of bowel movements.

The person who is used to having a bowel movement every day is likely to reach for a laxative if it does not occur. But, in doing so, he or she should be aware that various brands of commercial laxatives have very different effects. There are lubricant laxatives, stool-softening laxatives, saline laxatives, water retaining laxatives (including both enemas and suppositories), stimulant laxatives, and bulk-forming laxatives.

Stimulant laxatives are among the most widely used, and misused. While they can be efficacious if used occasionally and for short periods (not to exceed a week), physicians warn that prolonged use of stimulant laxatives can *create* chronic constipation because the system becomes dependent on the drug or combination of drugs present. Ask your druggist or physician if the drug you are buying is a stimulant laxative; among the most common ingredients in stimulant laxatives are phenolphtalein, danthron, aenna and bisacodyl. Castor oil is also a stimulant.

Bulk-forming laxatives are regarded as the safest. It is important, however, to drink at least an eight-ounce glass of water with each dose. Otherwise, the digestive tract may become obstructed. Bulk-forming laxatives usually contain derivatives of cellulose, psyllium or other such ingredients as bran or malt soup extract. But, physicians advise, there is really no need to purchase such special medications if your diet contains reasonable amounts of roughage in the form of whole-grain fiber, vegetables, and fruits. These, in themselves, are bulk-forming laxatives.

If you eat right, your system won't go wrong. If you have problems for a few days, let nature take its own course. A continuing problem means that you should consult your physician.

LEAD POISONING

The potential dangers of lead poisoning are not to be ignored or overlooked. Warnings on this subject have appeared regularly in the media for the past 15 years, laws have been passed to prevent the use of lead paint in homes, schools, and other facilities where young children congregate, but cases of lead poisoning still occur, often because people assume that the problem has been eradicated. It has not been. If you are moving into an apartment or house that still has layers of old paint, be certain to have chips analyzed. Young children who eat scrapings or chips of lead paint can become seriously ill; in some cases, irreversible brain damage can occur.

You should also be wary of the water system in your abode. Many old pipes are held together by lead soldering, which can introduce lead particles into your drinking water. There is, however, an easy precaution you can take if you suspect that lead soldering exists in the plumbing. The lead particles, experts say, accumulate overnight, when the water is not flowing regularly through the system. Therefore, if you run the water for two minutes in the morning before anyone drinks it, the lead content will be flushed out.

Don't rely exclusively on this precautionary measure. If you have any suspicion about the paint on your walls or the safety of your plumbing system, get it checked out. Now.

LEFT, RIGHT

Many left-handed people feel that their plight ought to have been addressed in antidiscrimination legislation. When they are growing up they get laughed at in school because they tend to hold a pen at a peculiar angle. There are all those disparaging remarks about people with two left feet. And some tools seem to have been designed to thwart them—scissors, for example (although there are left-handed scissors on the market).

For these and other reasons, many children are discouraged by parents and teachers from following their natural inclination to use the left hand. That's a mistake. Studies have shown that forcing a child to use his or her right hand can cause learning problems, including stuttering. That's because of the special functions of and the complex interrelation between the left and right halves of the brain.

It is estimated that nearly a third of the population would be left-handed if those people had been allowed to use the hand they naturally preferred. A lot of the best people have been left-handed. Your kid might grow up to be a Benjamin Franklin or a Pablo Picasso. Or a Bill Lee, the former Red Sox and Montreal Expos lefty pitcher who deserves to have the last word on the subject: "You have two hemispheres in your brain—a left and a right side. The left side controls the right side of your body and the right controls the left half. It's a fact. Therefore, left-handers are the only people in their right minds."

LEGAL LINGUISTICS

When confronted with the complex and nearly impenetrable language that infests so many legal documents, the average person often assumes that the lawyer knows what he or she is doing and, not wanting to appear ignorant, simply lets it pass.

This is absolutely the wrong way to deal with legal jargon. Every profession naturally develops its own special language, from plumbing (P-Trap—that's the U-shaped pipe under the sink), to cooking ("bain-marie"—that's when you put a dish containing such foods as pate into another pot containing simmering water). But there are certain professions and "disciplines" that seem to be particularly encumbered with jargon that is difficult for the rest of us to understand. Lawyers, doctors, psychiatrists, sociologists, and, more recently, computer developers, are among the champion obfuscators of all time.

There are three possible reasons why a member of one of these professions uses language you can't understand.

1. He or she couldn't get a degree without it, and its use has become a habit.
2. He or she hasn't really thought through what he or she is talking about, or simply doesn't know, and jargon is useful for papering over the cracks in a flawed argument or diagnosis.
3. If he or she turns out to be wrong, he or she can always hide behind the jargon and say, "that's not what I meant," which usually works because nobody else knows what is meant either.

The third point is the most important in dealing with legal documents. Loopholes. Members of Congress sit down and *purposely* create loopholes day in and day out. A loophole is there to give somebody an out, but it is unlikely to be you.

Anything that you do not understand in a legal document, of any sort, should be challenged immediately. Ask the lawyer to explain it to you in common English. If he or she can't do that, ask the lawyer to rewrite the clause or section so that it *is* understandable to you. If he or she can't do that, or refuses to do it, go elsewhere. If it can't be explained in plain English, then either it isn't worth explaining in the first place, or someone is trying to diddle you. When it comes to clarifying language, don't take no for an answer or, one way or another, you will end up being taken.

LETTERS TO THE EDITOR

All of us occasionally get the urge to write to a newspaper or magazine about some issue we care about deeply. We compose a letter to the editor in our heads. Usually, we don't bother to write it down, or having written it, think better of the whole thing and don't mail it. But what if you want to send that letter, and see it in print? What gives you the best chance of having it published?

First, you need to recognize that most publications print letters in keeping with their own style. Take a look at the Letters to the Editor column in the specific publication you want to send your thoughts or opinions to. Some tabloid-style newspapers, for example, seldom publish a letter that is longer than a few sentences. They may, on the other hand, welcome simple statements of opinion of a political or social nature that more "intellectual" publications are not interested in. You can write a tabloid that you think the president is doing a great job and that people who criticize him are left-wing bleeding hearts and/or right-wing zealots. But a mere statement of opinion of that sort won't get you in to the letters columns of "serious" newspapers like *The New York Times,* *The Washington Post,* or *The Los Angeles Times.* They publish considerably longer letters, but the letters must contain reasoned statements of fact (why you agree or disagree) and not mere judgments you might make to a neighbor over the back fence. If you have spotted an error of fact in a publication, can offer contrary or additional supporting evidence concerning an issue that has been discussed in the pages of a newspaper or magazine, or can suggest an interesting solution to a social or practical problem, your chances of having your letter published are very good.

Letters to the editor should be typed and must contain your name and address if you want them to be considered for publication. You can ask to have your name withheld, although few publications will print an anonymous letter unless there are very good reasons to do so (a comment from a rape victim, for example). If you are writing in response to a particular article, editorial, or letter that has appeared in the publication, cite the date that item appeared and identify it by title or author. A letter in response to an item that has actually appeared in print, by the way, is far more likely to be published than general comments on the world.

Last but not least, control your temper and watch your language. Mass-market publications are not interested in street language, nor do they look kindly on the potentiality of a libel suit. There are certain specialized literary and political periodicals in which lengthy, personal tirades fly back and forth in the letters columns for weeks or months, but you can only get away with that if you are already famous and can afford a good lawyer.

LIGHTNING STRIKES

It's a hot August day. You're at the beach, on the golf course, or playing softball in a field. Dark thunderclouds have been building up in the distance, but you've ignored them. Suddenly, the rain pours down and lightning strikes only a few hundred yards away. If you're on the golf course, or in an open field, you should never take shelter under a tree—that's the most dangerous thing you can do since the height of the tree makes a likely target for the lightning. The electrical discharge won't just strike the tree, however; it will continue right down to the ground, where you're standing.

What can you do? You can run for safe shelter, a building or a car. But if the lightning is close, that may be the wrong thing to do, especially if shelter is some distance away. Lightning can move with lightning speed. The first thing you should do is to divest yourself of any objects containing a lot of metal. That means your golf clubs, the portable radio you've taken to the beach, or your beach umbrella. Drop them, and get at least 50 feet away. Then, hit the ground. On a golf course, a sand trap is a good place to lie low—provided it isn't near a stream or water trap. At the beach, move away from the water and head for sand dunes or lie beside the boardwalk. In a field, hit the dirt at the flattest part of it, right out in the middle. And wherever you are, stay down until you are absolutely sure the lightning has passed on.

MAIL-ORDER MADNESS

The magazine ad or the brochure you receive in the mail may be offering copper pots, diamond earrings, digital watches, a pasta-making machine, and many other items. And the prices are so low—almost too good to be true. Well, they often are. The copper pots may be so thin that they virtually melt on the stove, the diamond earrings mere pinheads, the digital watches so badly made as to stop functioning in a month, or the pasta-making machine mere plastic and available at any dime store.

If the price is too good to be true, don't buy, consumer groups advise. There are, of course, many highly reputable companies that offer products for purchase by mail, but, while there may be some bargains, it is almost always the case that you get what you pay for.

One other word of caution: never send away for anything that isn't pictured as well as fully described.

MAKING AN ENTRANCE

Hollywood legend has it that when MGM was filming Claire Boothe's *The Women* in 1939, several of the leading ladies in its all-star cast went to extraordinary lengths to impress one another with their importance. Norma Shearer and Joan Crawford each had her own claims for the title of queen of the MGM lot; Rosalind Russell was a relative newcomer, but she had status because her husband, Frederick Brisson, had produced the original Broadway hit. Thus each day, the story goes, when the three ladies arrived at the set in their limousines, they would have the chauffeur check to see if the other two stars had arrived yet; if not, he was instructed to drive around a little so that an ultimate grand entrance could be contrived.

Arriving last (in other words late) at an event is still in vogue nearly a half century later as a way of making a smashing impression, but these days only superstars like Elizabeth Taylor or the very, very rich can get away with it. If anyone else tries this ploy, she (or he) is likely to be resented and to become the object of caustic remarks. One can, of course, wear eye-catching or startling clothes, but that can become a very expensive proposition. There is, however, a simple but effective alternative for those of us who are not superstars and cannot afford fabulous wardrobes.

This tip was passed on by a prominent New York party-goer, who, for obvious reasons, prefers to remain anonymous. "Arriving very late is crass." she says. "The right way to attract attention to yourself is to enter the room, take two steps forward, and then stand absolutely still for several seconds. The only thing you move is your head, turning it slowly in an arc, as though trying to decide if anyone there is actually worth knowing. Of course, if there are any steps leading down into the room, you must pause at the top of them. It works every time. Heads swivel to see who is important enough to actually stand still. As soon as someone starts coming toward you, to greet you, then you begin to move again. Smiling graciously, of course."

MARTINI LORE

The dry martini, for decades the cocktail of cocktails, slipped in popularity during the 1960s as the sales of scotch and vodka overtook that of gin. In the 1980s, both of these spirits are under heavy assault from white wine and sparkling waters. But, since anybody can mix a scotch and soda (although some definite preferences as to the amount of soda do exist) or pour out a glass of white wine (the degree of chilling is the controversial point here), let us look at the composition of that still very popular and ever-mysterious drink, the dry martini.

There are two main points of debate. The first concerns the proper proportion of gin to dry vermouth. Two to one in favor of gin? Very out of favor. Three to one, four to one, seven to one, all the way up to twenty to one—all have their proponents. There are also those who favor simply rinsing a glass with dry vermouth, pouring the vermouth back into the bottle and adding iced gin. It seems generally agreed, however, that the less vermouth you use, the better the quality of the gin must be. Or, to turn that around, if you buy cheap gin you will need more vermouth to soften it. Each martini lover, naturally, knows that the proportions he or she favors are exactly right.

The second main point of contention is whether the martini should be stirred or shaken. Some would have it that shaking "bruises the gin," but this is a myth. David A. Embury's *The Fine Art Of Mixing Drinks*, first published in 1948, contains an explanation of the difference between stirring and shaking that remains unmatched for clarity. And clarity is what it is all about. For many, Mr. Embury notes, one of the pleasures of a dry martini is the crystalline shimmer of it in the glass. If you want to preserve that clarity, he advises you to stir. Shaking a pitcher of martinis causes a "muddying" of the drink because of the properties of the vermouth. On the other hand, many people are more elated by a very cold martini than by its clarity. In that case, shake.

Right? Wrong? Martini making is an area in which people should *agree* to differ but usually just prefer to differ.

MASHED POTATOES

It's extraordinary how many otherwise decent cooks serve lumpy mashed potatoes. One way around that problem, of course, is to use that glutinous paste marked "instant." But there is a way to achieve smooth, flavorsome *real* mashed potatoes, and you can have them every time by following a few simple rules.

First, the potatoes themselves. The Idaho Potato Board recommends baking potatoes; and while they may be pushing their own major product, they happen to be right. Waxy new potatoes won't work. The baking potatoes should be scrubbed and boiled *in their skins*. If you peel them, you'll not only lose vitamins, but the potatoes will absorb water, increasing the possibility of lumps. Once the potatoes are tender, hold them on the end of a two-pronged fork and peel them quickly. If you have a ricer, which operates on the principle of a meat grinder, force the potatoes through it into the cooking pot and then return the pot to the stove, stirring over low heat for a moment before adding butter and milk. If you don't have a ricer, shake the potatoes over low heat briefly, to remove excess moisture, and then begin to mash. It's at this point that many people make a crucial mistake. Assuming that liquid will make the mashing easier, they add milk before or as they mash. It may make the mashing physically less taxing but it is guaranteed to cause lumps. The potatoes should be thoroughly mashed *before* any milk is added. Use a metal masher with multiple holes, not a fork. Once the potatoes are fairly smooth, add softened butter and continue mashing until there are no remaining lumps. Then gradually add *heated* milk until the desired consistency is acquired, and season with salt and pepper to taste.

MAYONNAISE MYSTERIES

Cookbook after cookbook decries the use of store-bought mayonnaise and urges making it in the home kitchen. It's so simple to make, the authors claim, and flavor and texture are so superior. All that's required is an egg yolk, some lemon juice or vinegar, a good olive oil, and a few minutes to whip up this delectable sauce. With a blender or food processor, they add, it's a breeze.

But it isn't. Many fine home cooks have tried to make mayonnaise and ended up with a sauce no thicker than heavy cream or, still worse, a curdled mess. The problem stems from the omission from the great majority of the best-selling cookbooks of the last two decades of a simple but crucial instruction.

Julia Child and the French food writer Raymond Oliver are two cookbook authors who provide, indeed insist upon, the crucial secret to making successful mayonnaise. It is this: *both* the egg yolks and the oil must be at the same room temperature. If you have cold oil or cold egg yolks, the yolks will not properly accept the oil that is being added to them. It's simply a matter of chemistry. If you've waited until the last minute, you can heat the oil very slightly, for a few seconds, and then let it cool to room temperature; in the case of cold eggs, you can rinse the mixing bowl with hot water and dry it thoroughly before adding the egg yolks. But room temperature to begin with is best.

MOUSETRAPS

The better mousetrap has yet to be invented, though they keep trying. There are plastic squares filled with glue. Mice step on the glue and are trapped. But then they drag the square around, twitching and squealing as they go and you've got to pick the trap up and throw the live mouse in the trash can. A lot of people get squeamish even reading about it.

There are also cage traps. You put bait in the cage, the mouse clambers in to get the food, and can't get out again. You've still got a live mouse to dispose of. Of course there's poison, which is fine if you have no children or pets and don't mind the stink behind your walls as the mice decay.

The old-fashioned spring trap, which usually kills the mouse at once, remains the most efficacious contraption. But what do you bait it with? Forget hard cheese. Smart mice can get the cheese off the trap without getting caught. A neighbor once watched a mouse move a pellet of dry dog food onto a trap, springing it; the mouse then scampered off with the cheese. Bacon also is easily dislodged by the intelligent mouse. You need something sticky and runny. A smeared dollop of processed cheese spread can work. But the ultimate in gourmet fare for a mouse appears to be peanut butter. Soft and sticky enough to adhere to the spring, and with an enticing aroma. Even smart mice are tempted. There are no guarantees of course, but peanut butter, according to numerous mousetrappers, has got the edge as bait.

MUGGERS' TARGETS

It is often said that anybody can get mugged. That's not untrue, but it obscures other important considerations. Law enforcement studies across the country have shown that certain kinds of people are much more likely than others to be assaulted on the street. In the course of their criminal careers, muggers develop instinctive "psychological profiles" of likely targets. Muggers are most likely to prey on people who seem tentative or timid, lost in thought, tipsy, or physically frail.

If you are worried about being mugged, and send out signals of your concern, appearing nervous, uncertain or downright afraid, you will simply increase the chances of an attack. The mugger knows that because of your fear, you are more likely to capitulate immediately, and turn over your possessions without resisting.

Even small or slight people, studies have shown, can reduce their chances of being mugged by walking with confidence and dispatch. Be aware of what is going on around you, but avoid constantly looking over your shoulder or giving other signs of nervousness. If you see people hanging out on the block ahead of you who seem dangerous, cross the street, but don't do it in a hurried or nervous way. Try to cross at a corner, and make it appear that that was your plan all along.

If, however, you feel certain you are being followed by a mugger, do not break into a run. Walk right out into the middle of the street, calling attention to yourself and making other people notice you. Even at night, muggers prefer to keep to the shadowy sides of a thoroughfare, where *they* feel safest.

MUSHROOM GATHERING

Of the earth's secret bounty, wild mushrooms can be one of the most delectable treats. They can also, of course, be poisonous, as deadly as botulism. This scares many people away from mushroom gathering altogether. But others take great pleasure in discovering a "fairy's ring" of mushrooms, or a patch of inky caps, shaggy manes, or wild morels growing in the shadows of the woods. And eating the mushrooms you've gathered can be perfectly safe, if you follow the rules.

Amateurs get into trouble because they think they know more than they really do. Some people assume that you can tell a safe mushroom by its coloration, whether of the cap or the gills beneath the cap. That assumption is wrong. Inky caps, for example, with their purplish triangular cap markings, look ominous but are harmless and delectable. The white *Amanita verna*, with its long slender stem and unmarked cap looks innocuous but is in fact one of the most deadly of poisonous mushrooms. Some mushrooms can fool even the expert. *Lepiota morgani* and *Lepiota rachodes* are related species, but the former is poisonous and the latter edible. When the poisonous variety is mature, its gills turn green, while the gills of the edible variety remain white—thus a distinction can be made. But this only works if the mushrooms have reached full maturity. When half grown, both varieties look exactly alike, and authorities therefore recommend avoiding even the edible *Lapiota rachodes* just to be safe.

There are also old wives' tales to deal with. Some people claim that a poisonous mushroom will turn a silver spoon or coin black if they are put into the pot with the mushrooms while they are cooking. This may work some of the time, but where poisonous mushrooms are concerned, some of the time isn't enough.

The best and safest way for theebeginner to approach the joys of mushroom gathering is to go out with someone who has wide knowledge and experience. That may be a professional botanist or simply a long-time local resident of an area who has been gathering wild mushrooms for years. You can also buy a book on mushrooms—*The Mushroom Pocket Field Guide* by Howard E. Bigelow (Collier Books, 1979) is a good one—and thoroughly familiarize yourself with the appearance and growing habits of a few common mushrooms. Puffballs, which look like oversized melons, can hardly be mistaken for anything else, and are delicious. Morels, with their elongated honeycomb caps, are also readily identifiable and perhaps the most delectable of all mushrooms. Shaggy manes are also easily recognized.

If you pick only those mushrooms you *know* to be edible, and avoid any that give you even the slightest doubt no matter how attractive they may appear, you can go mushroom gathering with perfect safety.

NOSEBLEEDS

How do you stop a nosebleed?

A great many people grab a handkerchief or tissue and press it to the nose, which is fine as far as it goes. But then they make the mistake of lying down or tilting the head back as far as possible. And that's the wrong approach.

Most medical reference books advise wetting a piece of cotton just large enough to fit in the nostril (a piece of wet tissue can be used if there's no cotton available) and inserting it in the nostril. Using your thumb and forefinger, you should then apply pressure on both sides of the nose. But this should be done sitting up, not lying down. Why? Because if you lie down the blood is likely to seek another escape route and run down into your throat through the interior nasal passages. Thus instead of stenching the flow, you will merely divert it to another channel. Continue the pressure on the nose, sitting up, for three or four minutes. If that doesn't stop the bleeding, try again with a larger piece of cotton. Beyond that, call a physician.

Minor nosebleeds can have a number of causes. It may be simple dryness. Changes in pressure, whether from flying in a plane, taking an elevator to a high floor, or making a deep dive into water, can bring on a nosebleed. Children may cause nosebleeds by picking their noses. Even a mild bang to the head may bring on a nosebleed some time after the event.

Recurrent nosebleeds should be brought to the attention of a physician. They may be an indication of high blood pressure or some other medical condition. Since most nosebleeds are from veins, even fairly severe recurrent nosebleeds can be easily rectified by local cauterizing. But a recurrent condition may be a warning sign of a tumor or some other disease and should be fully investigated.

NUTRITION NOTIONS

Outside of astrophysics, the most controversial area of scientific pursuit in recent years is unquestionably nutrition, the study of the effects on our health of the foods we eat. Television talk shows often feature nutritionists engaged in health debates, which sometimes boil over into screaming matches. That there should be so much controversy is hardly surprising. Nutrition is, after all, a very new field taken seriously by scientists and physicians only since the 1930s.

That is why we have influential, best-selling "diet doctors" who recommend a weight-loss program based on the intake of 600 calories a day, while others flatly state that anything less than 1,200 calories a day is detrimental to our health. That is why even the most extensive studies on the dangers of cholesterol are debunked by other researchers who claim that it is impossible to come to any real conclusions about cholesterol without studies conducted over at least a fifty-year period and recording every single item that at least 30,000 people eat in that time. That is also why some physicians recommend large doses of vitamins in pill form, while others are convinced that the vitamin craze is being promoted by profit-hungry drug companies.

About the only things the "experts" agree on is that most Americans consume too much sugar and salt and not enough fiber. Beyond that, the main business of many physicians and nutritionists appears to be questioning one another's credentials and research techniques.

Who's the ordinary person supposed to believe? The answer, for the time being anyway, is himself or herself. Given how polarized the science of nutrition is at the present time, it's a sure bet that someday certain scientists will come up with conclusive evidence for their positions, proving the opposition wrong. Meanwhile, perhaps the best thing for us to do is inform ourselves about all sides of a given nutritional issue and use our own judgment. The odds are that the fad diets and food crazes will pass and that moderation will continue to be the safest and healthiest course, as it has been for thousands of years.

OBSCENE PHONE CALLS

A woman of the author's acquaintance picked up the telephone one evening and a male voice said, "Hello, is this Lucy?"

"Yes."

"Well, this is an obscene phone call."

"Okay," said Lucy, "Hold on a minute while I get my cigarettes."

In this case the ploy worked. Obscene phone calls are a form of long distance assault, and those who make them are not looking for cooperation, as a rule. On the other hand, you could make an unwanted friend, and such unorthodox approaches are not recommended.

What does work? Telephone companies, which take obscene and harassing calls very seriously, recommend that you hang up quietly at the first obscene word or if the caller doesn't answer the second time you say hello. Don't slam down the phone or shout angrily at the caller: this may be exactly the response the caller was hoping for. No reaction is the best reaction. And never give out any information until a caller has been identified. Be sure to teach your children how to react to such situations. In the case of persistent calls, contact your telephone company's Annoyance Call Bureau, which will enlist the help of the police if necessary.

There are also steps you can take of a precautionary nature. Having a loud whistle on hand to blow through the mouthpiece can work, but experts warn that it can also make the caller angry enough to cause further problems. If you are a woman living alone, it may be wise to have your name listed in the telephone book using initials only, although some of those who make obscene calls take initials as a challenge and give it a try. You might want to have a male friend with an authoritative voice make a brief tape—no more than a sentence or two—which can be played if a caller persists, telling him succinctly to get lost. You can also do that yourself if you refuse to be intimidated. But do it firmly and quietly. Finally, telephone companies advise against telling neighbors or friends about obscene calls; many are made by people who know you, and word of your concern may encourage the caller.

ONION PEELS

Some onions are more likely than others to make you cry when you peel or chop them: it depends on their variety and age; older onions are most potent. An old-fashioned remedy for onion tears is to hold a piece of bread crust between your teeth as you work, but many people find this approach thoroughly unpalatable, since the bread inevitably turns soggy in the mouth.

It is helpful to know that the tears are caused not by the onion flesh itself, but by the thin translucent layer that lies just under the parchment-like outer skin. If you cut off the top and bottom of the onion and then remove the outer skin and the translucent layer beneath cold running water, your tears should be stayed. Be advised, though, that large Spanish onions, of the kind used for making onion rings, may have several translucent membranes at intervals. Slice the onions rapidly, in this case, putting the complete rounds immediately into a bowl of cold water, and then separate the individual rings under running water.

OUTDOOR WIRING

Guests are coming to dinner. You've spruced up the house and watered the lawn. Then, 20 minutes before the guests are due to arrive, the bulb burns out in the wrought-iron lantern at the end of your driveway. Annoying, but easily remedied. You grab a light bulb from the closet and head out to restore illumination, flicking off the switch for the lantern as you go.

STOP! Don't take another step. As any professional electrician will tell you, you could be in serious danger of electrocution. That grass may still be damp. And even though the switch is off, you can't take too many precautions when it comes to outdoor electrical wiring.

Electricians urge that any outdoor wiring be on a different circuit from that which feeds power to the interior of your house. That way, you can easily switch off the outdoor circuit without disrupting interior usage. Even if you're only going to change a light bulb, switch off the entire outdoor circuit first.

You should also be aware that a device called a ground fault interrupter is required by law on all outdoor wiring. It's designed to monitor the current and to shut down all power in approximately 1/35th of a second if a leak occurs. If you're buying a new house or putting in outdoor lighting, make sure a ground fault interrupter exists or is installed.

Finally, if you want to install any kind of electrical wiring around a swimming pool, hire a professional electrician. That's no job for the do-it-yourselfer. The slightest short circuit could electrocute anyone who touches the water.

OVEN FIRES

Oven fires, especially in gas ovens, can be extremely dangerous. The first thing to do is to turn off the oven. The best way to put the fire out is with a small household fire extinguisher, but do not open the oven door until you have the extinguisher in your hand. The last thing you should use is water, which can cause the grease in the oven to spatter wildly. Instead, use salt, large quantities of it. Keep on hand an emergency box of salt, just for this purpose. Don't try pouring the salt into your bare hands and throwing it in. Instead, empty the salt into a long handled pot, which will allow you to stand back from the oven while you douse the flames.

You are far less likely to have an oven fire in the first place if you clean your oven regularly.

OVERDUE BILLS

The worst thing you can do with an overdue bill is to stick it in a drawer and try to forget it. Somebody is remembering. At first, for one month or two depending upon the company, agency or organization, it will be a computer doing the remembering. But then that bill is going to turn up on some person's desk, and matters will begin to get serious. Even if you can't pay the bill, it is better to telephone before the debt comes to the attention of an individual or gets referred to a collection agency. Explain your problem, state when you are likely to be able to pay at least part of the bill, and the matter is likely to be turned back to the computer—or retained in it—at least for a while.

What you have to realize is that the whole country, indeed the entire globe, is in over its financial head. If all the overdue bills were called up at once, the entire system would collapse of its own weight. Your creditors become worried, though, when they get no reply whatsoever. Are you still alive? Have you skipped the town or the country? So long as they know you are still breathing, and are trying to take care of the problem, they relax a little.

So far as your creditors are concerned, even bad news ("I can't pay until the end of the month") is better than no news.

OVERSEXED PLANTS

You are starting a flower garden and friends and neighbors are helping you out with gifts. They've provided you with violas, the campanula known as bluebells of Scotland, lily of the valley, a bleeding heart of the luxuriant variety, some fresh-smelling mint. Your little niece has even contributed a packet of morning-glory seeds. How marvelous, you think.

Well, beware. Your niece may not know any better, but your friends and neighbors have presented you with all the rampantly spreading plants that have overrun their own gardens. The whole lot of them are dreadfully oversexed and reproduce as do such weeds as dandelions and crabgrass. The bleeding heart will be the easiest to control, because although it will drop babies in every direction, they are shallow-rooted and can be easily disposed of. Not so the bluebells, the violas, the lily of the valley, and the mint, however. They spread and spread and spread, and it's almost impossible to eradicate them completely. As they spread, they crowd out more delicate and more glamorous flowers, as well as suck water and nutrients out of the soil at a great rate. They may be pretty and they may smell nice, but be prepared for annual guerrilla warfare to keep them in check.

As to morning glories, they are indeed glorious, but don't plant them near any other flower or bush—their tendrils will entwine themselves around anything within reach.

OYSTER SHUCKING

Bluepoints. Chincoteagues. Cotuits. The Colchesters of England and the Belons of Brittany. Oysters all, varying in size and flavor, each with its own devotees. The true oyster lover prefers them raw, on the half shell. But even if you like them cooked—fried, in oyster stew, or as "angels on horseback," wrapped in bacon and broiled—you still have to get the shells open. If you're going to cook them, you can buy them already shucked at the fish market—make sure the liquid is clear and not milky—but even for cooking, the fresher they are the better they are. If you're planning to offer them raw on the half shell, you must open them yourself at the last minute.

Many people make the mistake of trying to shuck oysters with knives that are too long and too sharp. A knife that's too long will decrease your leverage. A knife that's too sharp can cause a bad cut. This is one case where you need to invest in a special piece of equipment if you want to do the job right: a short, thick-bladed, and round-nosed oyster knife.

Fishing expert A. J. McClane and the old hands of the Grand Central

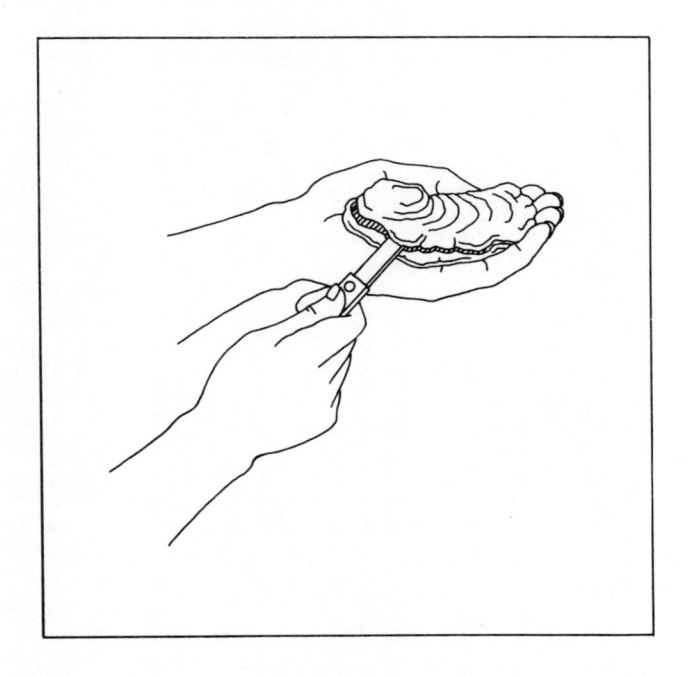

Oyster Bar and Restaurant of New York recommend basically similar procedures, the major difference being in how the oyster is held. Either you grasp the oyster in the palm of your hand or you rest it on a table or counter top and hold it in place with your hand. The tabletop approach might seem safer to the neophyte, but fishmongers and fishermen in general feel you get greater control if you grip it tightly in your palm.

Whichever method you choose, the thin end of the oyster should point toward you, with the hinge of the shells against your hand. Push the blade of the oyster knife between the two shells close to the hinge. Then run the blade away from you with a twisting motion to cut the oyster's abductor muscle that holds the valves together.

Now you have an oyster on the half shell. If you get really adept, you can enter one of the oyster-shucking contests that take place annually all along the oyster coasts of North America and Europe. The record to beat is 100 oysters in under four minutes.

PACKAGE TOURS

The package tour was originally invented for the tourist who was afraid to travel abroad alone and has thus been the butt of many jokes—there was even a Hollywood movie called *If It's Tuesday, This Must Be Belgium*. And there are countries, such as the Soviet Union and China, that will not allow the average tourist to visit except as a member of a government-controlled package tour.

Over the years, however, the range and interest of possible package tours has increased enormously. There are now many tours available that take care of the travel and lodging essentials but leave you free to wander and explore on your own, away from the group, for anything from several hours to several days. Many such tours include an initial orientation tour of the city you are visiting and give you the security of knowing that you can fall back on tour organizers in the event of confusion. At the same time, you can shop at your leisure, eat some meals in indigenous restaurants rather than hotel dining rooms or tourist traps, and seek out museums or sights that are of special interest to you but would not be on the itinerary of a group tour. This kind of half-and-half package tour may be the ideal compromise for the first-time visitor to a foreign country, or elderly travelers who don't want to deal with the more mundane hassles of traveling but retain a spirit of adventure.

Just one word of caution: stay away from tours that try to encompass too much too quickly.

PAPER TRAINING

In cities, many veterinarians advise against walking your new puppy outside until it has had its final shots—usually after about three months—in order to prevent the dog from picking up diseases. That means paper training your puppy. Females are more easily paper trained than males in most cases, but you can have success with either sex if you go about it right.

It is essential that someone be at home regularly during the paper-training period. Begin by showing your puppy where the papers are. Keep an eye on the dog. Any time you see it squat, whether to urinate or defecate, pick the puppy up immediately and carry it to the newspapers and place the dog on them. This can be messy, since the dog may continue to void while you are carrying it. But dealing with a little mess at the beginning can save you endless trouble in the long run. There is no need to spank the dog. If it is carried to the papers each time it begins to "do its business," it will begin to associate that activity with the papers.

If the dog makes a mess while your back is turned, take the dog to the place where it has urinated or defecated, hold its head down so that it can smell the waste (do *not* actually rub its nose in it), say, "No," and then carry the dog to its papers and say, "Good dog." If the dog has defecated, scoop up the stools and place them on the papers, showing the dog that that is where they belong.

Once your dog gets the idea, be sure to praise it every time it does use the papers. It may continue to make the occasional mistake, but once it has begun to do things right, praise becomes more important than censure.

PARROT TALK

Some parrots are superstars. There's a California parrot that has really made it, appearing on *The Tonight Show* and national news programs, all decked out in green feathers Phyllis Diller would envy, to offer a haunting rendition of "San Francisco."

Other parrots are a bit slow; many are given to juvenile delinquency. Pet shop owners will tell you that any parrot can be taught to talk, but they give no guarantees, and they emphasize the word "taught." Thus many parrots just perch in their cages and squawk unintelligibly, especially when you are on the telephone. Others have no use for grammar or complete sentences, but will pick up and repeat any dirty word ever uttered in their presence—perhaps because those words were spoken with such profound feeling, emphasis, and volume.

Some parrots are extremely polite. A woman who spent a week visiting old friends who owned an ancient and generally rather reticent parrot, came downstairs early one morning, before anyone else was up, to make herself some coffee. As she passed through the dining room on the way to the kitchen, a voice greeted her from the corner of the room: "Good morning, Georgia," it said. "Good morning, Georgia." Georgia jumped about ten feet and then realized that it was just old Wilbur, taking upon himself the duties of host.

You can teach parrots to do amazing things with their voices. But you will have to spend a lot of time at it, be very patient, reward the bird for excellence, and generally treat it as though it were your only child. If you do so, you are likely to find that, like a child, it will begin to speak its own mind.

PASSPORT APPLICATIONS

Every year, during late spring and early summer, long lines of panicky people form at each of the 13 United States Passport Agencies in Boston, Chicago, Honolulu, Houston, Los Angeles, Miami, New Orleans, New York, Philadelphia, San Francisco, Seattle, Stamford, or Washington, D.C. They are people who are planning a trip abroad, and they need a passport, fast. Either they've never had one before, or their old passport has expired. Sometimes they wait in line for hours, having taken the day off from work, only to be told that they might as well go home because they'll never get to the front of the line before the office closes. Anger abruptly overrides panic.

Even if they do get to the front of the line, they may find that they haven't brought the necessary documents or the proper photographs that are required for the processing of a passport. It's a mess. But it is really their fault, not that of the Department of State's Passport Agency.

The major problem is procrastination. The applicant's procrastination. The instructions on the back of the single-page passport application are topped by two statements set off by heavy arrows: "Don't Put It Off. Apply Now." and "Avoid The Last Minute Rush." But applicants do put it off and cause both themselves and the Passport Agency endless problems by doing so.

It generally takes four to five weeks to process a passport; in emergencies, that can be speeded up, cut to two weeks or even a matter of days. But if such an emergency arises, you are going to need more documents to convince the passport agency that it really is an urgent matter—your plane tickets, for example. Passport officials urge you to *apply now* if there's a chance you might be traveling abroad for any reason—pleasure, business, or visiting relatives. It is going to cost you more than $35 at this writing, but that fee is likely to go up, and since passports for adults are now valid for 10 years (five years if you are under 17), you can call it an investment. It is also the best kind of identification you can have. Don't wait.

Then there is the form itself. It is actually a very simple form. There are fewer lines to fill out than appear on the short income tax form. But you do have to fill them out. You must know your father and mother's birthplace. Or, if you don't know, and can't find out, be prepared to give a good reason why not. You must have a birth certificate, and getting one may take a while, another reason for applying well ahead of time. If no birth record exists or you were born out of the United States, there are alternative application procedures; obtain a form and find out what special documents you will need to give proof of citizenship. It's helpful to know that the application is available not just at Passport Agency offices, but also at hundreds of post offices across the country, where specially trained postal officials can answer your questions and send your application on its way. It's very often easier to take advantage of their services than to line up at a passport office.

Finally we come to your photograph. The application instructions are very specific on what you need: "Submit two identical photographs of you alone, sufficiently recent to be a good likeness (normally taken within the last 6 months), 2 X 2 inches in size, with an image size from bottom of chin to top of head (including hair) of between 1 and 1 3/8 inches. Photographs must be clear, front view, full face, taken in normal street attire without a hat or dark glasses . . ."

Some people find these instructions almost funny. But they are there because people do have their photographs taken with hats and dark glasses, or submit two different photographs. The agency also tells you explicitly that snapshots, most vending machine prints, or full-length photographs are unacceptable. Still, people go on bringing them in.

The photographs can be in black-and-white or color, but they have to be printed on thin paper and able to withstand a temperature of 225 degrees during mounting. If you usually wear glasses, don't take them off so you'll look "good" in your passport photograph. Nobody ever looks good in a passport photograph; stop worrying about it and go get your picture taken by one of those little shops that specializes in them.

Getting a passport is easy if you give yourself enough time and follow instructions.

PATENT PENDING

The U.S. Department of Commerce issues in the neighborhood of 70,000 patents each year. Even so, there is a tremendous backlog of cases to be reviewed, which is why you see so many products with the statement "Patent Pending." As soon as you apply for a patent, however, you are protected. Even if somebody else comes in two days later with the same idea, you will ultimately get the patent if you applied for it first.

There are a few inventive people whose patents number in the hundreds. There are also some surprises. Who would guess that a patent was once issued to Mark Twain—for an improved variety of suspenders. You can get a patent for something that is truly new or for something that is merely a modification. So long as its design has not been previously patented, you own the rights.

But if you think you might get rich from inventing a better mousetrap, don't get your hopes up too high. It's been estimated that as many as 90 percent of the inventions patented by individuals, as opposed to companies, never even get manufactured. There are several reasons for that. Some inventions are too specialized, or expensive to manufacture, or just plain goofy to have a chance in the marketplace. In addition, most American companies are loath to buy the rights to an invention not produced by their own researchers. If you've got an invention you really believe in, your best bet may be to found your own company. That's what the inventor of a newfangled ice-cream maker did 30 years ago. His name was Tom Carvel.

PERFORMING KIDS

"Don't put your daughter on the stage, Mrs. Worthington," Noel Coward admonished in a lyric. No one seems to be paying Mr. Coward much mind. These days performing children are everywhere, from Broadway shows to television commercials.

Performing kids make lots of money, but don't think you're going to get rich off your moppet. Three-quarters of what they earn has to be held in trust until they reach age 18, the result of the famous Jackie Coogan law, passed after it was discovered that Coogan's mother had ripped off his entire fortune. Still, they'll be able to pay for their own college education if they drop out of show business, as a majority of performing kids do.

The various entertainment uniins have a warning for you, however. Never pay an "agent" an up-front fee to get your child on the stage or into films or commercials. Legitimate agents are entitled to a fee for their work, usually ten percent, but an agent who asks you for a "deposit," is a con artist out to bilk unwary parents. The agent gets his or her fee *after* the paychecks start rolling in, not before. Don't be overly upset if an agent refuses to represent your child. There are many who would say that turning people away is the favorite pastime of a legitimate agent.

PET PRIMACY

We all know people who seem to be obsessed with the welfare of their pets. They hesitate about accepting any invitation because it may interfere with the pet's feeding schedule; they rush out of dinner parties early because the dog needs to be walked or the cat is lonely; they seem to spend an extraordinary amount of time (and money) at the veterinarian's. These people, in your opinion, are clearly neurotic.

You may be quite wrong. In fact, their pets may be a great help in keeping them psychologically healthy.

Recent studies have shown that people with pets—especially single or elderly people—are less likely to experience loneliness or depression, are physically healthier, and often live longer than people who do not have pets. Psychologists point to a number of reasons why this should be so. Having a pet means that you have a living presence to come home to, a creature to care for, a creature that responds to and cares for you. Owning a dog, in particular, can actually increase your contact with other people: two strangers out walking their dogs think nothing of striking up a conversation while their pets sniff one another over. If there were no dog, the same people would have passed one another by without speaking. Most important, though, is that having a pet gives the owner who lives alone a responsibility to a living being outside himself or herself. The exercising of that responsibility may be an antidote to the loneliness or depression that the person might otherwise succumb to.

Of course, there *are* HIGHLY NEUROTIC PEOPLE WHO ALSO HAVE PETS. Those pets are likely to be neurotic, too, and badly behaved. The cat that tears furniture to shreds, the dog that howls every time its master goes out or regularly makes a mess in the middle of the living room floor, is an unhappy and badly trained pet. But then, as the renowned British dog trainer, Barbara Woodhouse, repeatedly insists: training an animal is easy; it's the owners that are the problem.

PHOTOGRAPHING KIDS

There are undoubtedly more bad photographs of young children than of any other subject in the world. Just look at your own family albums. Your rambunctious four-year-old son looks stiff and bored, your adorable five-year-old daughter has replaced her usual angelic smile with a baleful grimace. Or the picture is blurred—your kid moved just as you snapped the shutter.

More often than not, what you've done wrong is to ask your kid to *pose*.

Take a tip from professional photographers: give the child something to play with or something to eat. The child under six will be much happier and more relaxed if you allow him or her to get lost in a private little world, pushing the toy car around or digging into the paper cup of ice cream. You should never admonish a child to sit up straight, keep the hands still, raise the head, or smile. The less the child is aware of your presence, the better your picture will turn out.

Aaron Sussman, author of *The Amateur Photographer's Handbook*, (Crowell, 1973), suggests that if you expect to get good pictures of young children, you should be prepared to use a lot of film. He also advises using a very fast shutter speed, at least 1/100 if the child is sitting in one place, even faster if the child is involved in an activity such as playing by the water's edge or bouncing a ball. The fast shutter speed allows for the capture of the sudden movement on the child's part that may be the most characteristic expression of his personality.

Using patience, plenty of film, and allowing the child to amuse himself or herself will get you the kinds of pictures you want of your kids.

PICTURE HANGING

Picture hanging is a difficult chore. You can all too easily end up with falling plaster, holes in the wall, and a picture that is too high, too low, or crooked. Some chic young interior designers have lately gotten around the issue altogether by leaning pictures against the wall at floor level. This is fine, provided you have no children or pets, don't really want anyone to look at your pictures anyway, and won't be upset if someone puts a foot through the glass at a cocktail party.

Most of us, however, want our pictures on the wall. The first thing to remember, both museum curators and traditional interior designers advise, is that if the painting or photograph is worth looking at in the first place, it should be hung at eye level. For those of average height, eye-level means that the center of the picture should be between five and six feet off the ground. You might want to hang the occasional picture higher than that, as an accent, but the picture chosen should be bold enough in color or design so that it can still be clearly viewed. A wall of small pictures or photographs hung one above the other can be effective, but the lowest shouldn't be below four feet from the ground, or the highest more than seven feet.

What about the actual hanging process? Newspaper columnists, syndicated features like "Mary Ellen's Helpful Hints," and local handyman experts suggest such tricks as cutting out a paper pattern and tacking it to the wall with thumbtacks, using a level, and scotch-taping the wall where the nail is to be driven in to avoid too large a hole. All good suggestions. But the real answer is that it takes at least two people to hang a picture properly. Bernard X. Woolf, who has installed exhibitions at many major museums, wouldn't think of hanging a picture without the participation of two, three or even four people, depending on the size and weight of the painting. So, if you want to succeed at getting a picture up on the wall at the proper height and hanging straight, be sure to involve your spouse, children, friends, and lovers. Do not enlist your children if they are under 16, however—they will insist that everything is too high.

POISON ALERT

A child has swallowed a dangerous cleaning product or pest-control substance; an adult has taken an overdose of pills or other drugs. What's the first thing you do?
  A. Induce vomiting in the victim.
  B. Call an ambulance.
  C. Contact your nearest Poison Control Center.
  The right answer is C.

Vomiting should never be induced as a *first* step, since there are many poisonous substances that can cause even more harm if they are brought back up through the system without special medical supervision.

But why not call an ambulance immediately? Because an ambulance, unfortunately, can take considerable time to reach you, especially in big cities or rural areas. What you do *before* the ambulance gets there may be a matter of life and death. The purpose of the Poison Control Center is to tell you what to do at once. There are more than 25 such regional centers in the United States, as well as many smaller ones associated with hospitals but listed separately in the telephone book under Poison Control. It's an emergency number you should have listed along with those for the police and the fire department. If there is no local Poison Control Center in your community, get the number of the nearest regional office, even if it's in another state. The centers don't care where the call is coming from—they're there to help.

They will want to know what poison or drug has been ingested. If there's a cleaning product that a child has been playing with, an empty bottle of pills or whatever, give them the name. Poison Control centers have extensive cross-referencing indexes that make it possible for them to identify the poisonous effects of hundreds of potentially harmful products, as well as the right way to deal with particular types of poisoning.

If you do not know what product or drug has caused the victim to become ill, you will be asked to describe symptoms. Again, a cross-referencing system will be used to advise you on what steps to take. As to that ambulance, the Poison Control Center will call one for you at your request. By calling the Poison Control Center first, you will know what to do while waiting for the ambulance and will be able to pass that information on immediately to the ambulance attendants. And knowing may save someone's life.

POISON IVY RELIEF

Some people can tear poison ivy out of the ground with their bare hands with no effect whatsoever. Others have only to brush up against the plant to become afflicted with itchy and eventually running sores. It's an allergic reaction. If you are allergic, there are precautions you can take, but no absolute preventive exists.

In terms of precautions:

1. Learn to recognize the plant, which is low growing, seldom attaining more than a foot in height, and has three pointed semiglossy dark green leaves to each stem.
2. Wear protective clothing in any area, from fields to woods to your own backyard, in which plants may have taken root.
3. Recognize that if you have a cat or dog that is allowed to roam freely, it may be carrying poison ivy allergens on its fur. They won't harm the animal, but if you are particularly susceptible, you could become infected simply from petting it. If you have contracted poison ivy and don't know why, give your pet a bath.

In terms of treatment:

1. Do not wash the affected area vigorously. It will make the problem worse by further irritating the skin. Instead, soak pieces of cloth in a mild solution of bicarbonate of soda or salt and apply them to the rash several times a day.
2. The application of calamine lotion or zinc oxide may help dry up the sores, thus preventing scratching. Scratching will not spread the rash to other parts of the body, contrary to what many people believe, but it will slow down the healing process.

POLLUTION AT HOME

We're all aware that the air in our cities (and even many small towns near industrial plants) is heavily polluted. Recent legislation has in some cases improved the atmosphere, but all too often the controls have only prevented the situation from getting worse.

You may feel, therefore, that you are often better off inside your well-insulated and air-conditioned house than outdoors in many areas. You could, unfortunately, be quite wrong.

A report carried out by the chemical hazards office of the Consumer Product Safety Commission concluded in 1984 that air pollution inside American homes may be ten times worse than outdoors. Such major pollutants as carbon dioxide and monoxide, sulfur dioxide, solvents, asbestos, plastics, pesticides, smoke, chloroform, and benzene were commonly present. Because formaldehyde is increasingly used in treating plywood and particle construction board materials, it has also become a growing problem. Aerosol sprays, the chemicals emanating from dry-cleaned fabrics, even cosmetics, add to the dangers.

The problem in part lies in the fact that the better insulated your house is, the more completely the pollutants are trapped indoors. There are some small steps you can take to improve the situation. Keep the windows open while using oven sprays or heavy cleaning fluids, and open them following the use of a bug spray. Remember that while room deodorizers may make things smell better, you are still releasing more chemicals into the air. If possible, hang dry-cleaned clothes outdoors for an hour or so before putting them away in a closet.

Always remember that the outside air, even if polluted, is fresher than that in your house. Open those windows!

POT POLITESSE

Pot smokers think they are being hospitable when they offer around a joint at a party. They forget that marijuana is illegal, and that there may be people present who are going to be made extremely nervous by this act of generosity. If you smoke pot, that's your business, but never offer it around at a gathering in someone else's home unless you are certain nobody is going to be offended or upset. That's mere politesse.

POWER MOWERS

Power mowers are a great boon to easy care of the suburban lawn. They also cut off people's toes. Elaine Zayak, the former world figure-skating champion, took up the sport as a form of rehabilitation after losing two toes as a child. No one should ever be barefoot, or wear open toed sandals around a power mower. You also need to be careful when using the hand-held electric mowers that employ revolving plastic cord. If the exposed length of the cord is too long, pieces of it can be cut off and fly through the air with great force, gashing your leg or causing other injury. Mowing the lawn is still a job, and you should wear work clothes when doing it, not bathing suits or skimpy clothing that leaves you exposed to potential harm.

PRESCRIPTION PASS-ONS

Jane is telling her friend Susan about the problems she's having with the latest man in her life. She finally bursts into tears and says "I'm just a wreck."

"Here," says Susan, reaching for her purse, "have one of my tranquilizers."

Susan is only trying to be helpful, but what she is doing is wrong, and it would be foolish of Jane to accept the offer.

There is a reason why your name is printed on the label of any prescription drug you buy. It was prescribed for you and only you. Physicians can't emphasize that too much. There are several kinds of prescription tranquilizers available, each of which may have a somewhat different effect upon given individuals. Some tranquilizers cause dizziness in some people and could make an already distraught person feel even worse.

Other drugs could be deadly if given to the wrong person. Antibiotics are a case in point. It is well known that some people are highly allergic to penicillin, but even some of the substitute antibiotics that have been developed can cause severe reactions, including convulsions, in a small minority of people.

No prescription drug should ever be passed on to anyone else.

PRIVATE DETECTIVES

Private detectives make most people think of Dashiell Hammett and Mickey Spillane, Humphrey Bogart movies, and a slew of television shows. Somehow, private detectives seem more fictional than real. But this is not the case. Check your Yellow Pages under Investigators, and you'll find, in large cities, dozens of private detective agencies listed.

The ads are provocative. "Matrimonial Investigations. Where They Went. What They Did. With Whom, Etc. Video and Telephoto Proof." Missing persons are traced and custody cases handled.

It sounds lurid, but private investigators can be helpful, even necessary in some situations. Make certain, however, before hiring one, that the agency is both licensed and bonded. Many agencies offer free consultations. Use such a consultation to get full information on costs, in writing. And remember, if a private investigator is going to do his or her job, he or she is not only going to need a lot of information about the person you want trailed, found, or investigated but is also going to want, or will discover, a great deal about *you*. Private in this case really means "independent." Yes, the information gathered will be held in confidence, but you must be prepared to have your privacy invaded.

PUTTING PROFICIENCY

The television commentators covering golf tournaments love to analyze the putting stance of individual golfers. There are close-ups of the way the golfer's hands are placed and of the putting head as it is measured against the ball. You watch closely and try to pick up pointers.

But perhaps you needn't bother. Almost all professional golfers will agree that putting is the most difficult aspect of the game and that most championships are decided on the putting green rather than on the fairways. But that's where the agreement ends. Take a look at half a dozen instructional books by famous golfers, and you'll discover that each champion, male or female, has a special approach to putting. Some emphasize the grip on the putting iron, others the position of the feet. Some say it is all in the wrists while others believe that although the body and head should not move unduly, a certain amount of overall follow-through movement is necessary.

Obviously, there is no single formula for successful putting. For that very reason, you may be hampering your development as a putter by trying to imitate or "learn" the technique used by a favorite professional golfer. There's no reason not to experiment, but perhaps the best overall advice comes from such champions as Bobby Jones and Billy Casper, who emphasize the individuality of golf in all its aspects. Bobby Jones has said, "The main thing is to be comfortable, thoroughly relaxed, with no hint of strain." And how do you do that? Listen to Billy Casper: "Within the framework of the fundamentals, find something that feels good to you."

QUEASY TRAVELERS

The symptoms of motion sickness are nausea and vomiting, but the cause is all in your head, whether figuratively or literally. In some cases, motion sickness is psychological, brought on by anxiety. This is especially likely to be true among children, who can become overexcited or fearful during a long trip, and those who have a phobia, as in "fear of flying." Motion sickness can also be due to inner-ear problems. The most important center of balance (or equilibrium) is situated in the inner ear. A person with motion sickness will often feel much better lying down because he or she has restored his sense of balance.

Over-the-counter motion sickness drugs (antiemetics) can help to control the nausea, but they should not be taken in combination with alcohol or other drugs, especially tranquilizers. And since they frequently cause drowsiness, one should never take them while driving.

QUESTIONS FOR CALL-INS

Radio and television call-in programs are all over the airwaves these days. Any metropolitan area is likely to have several of them. All you have to do is pick up your telephone, dial the special number given out by the announcer, and you can get your questions about sports, child psychology, sexual problems, gardening, or household repairs answered on the air by an expert in the field. Not all incoming calls are taken, of course. Dr. Judith B. Kuriansky, a clinical psychologist and sex therapist with a top-rated call-in show on New York's WOR radio station, notes that a lot of good questions don't get through to her because people don't understand the protocol involved.

When you telephone a live talk show, a producer or assistant will take the call and ask you several questions as part of a screening process. They're likely to ask where you are calling from, what your first name is, and the nature of your question. The reason for the first question is that if you're calling long distance, they'll try to get you on sooner. Your first name is asked to test whether or not you're really willing to be forthcoming, and because the host will ask you the same question to establish a more friendly context. The nature of your question is asked in order to avoid prank callers and weirdos. You will also be asked to turn down or turn off your home radio or television set. That's because, once you are on the air, the "echo" of your conversation in the background would be distracting both to you and to the host who's trying to answer your question.

If you've got a good question and are aware of the above protocol, you have an excellent chance of getting on the air.

RARE BOOKS

Does the fact that a book is a first edition make it rare? Not necessarily.

Does a beautiful, hand-tooled antique leather binding make a book rare? Seldom in and of it itself.

Does the fact that the book has been autographed by its author make a book rare? That depends on the author.

Does the fact that a book is one of a specially numbered edition make it rare? Not if the numbered edition was a large one. The smaller the number of copies printed, the more likely the book is to qualify as rare.

What makes a rare book rare is a combination of two factors: scarcity and demand.

A first edition of Herman Melville's *Moby Dick* would be worth a small fortune. A first edition of a forgotten novel by some obscure contemporary of Melville's would be worthless. A first edition of Hemingway's *The Sun Also Rises*, which had a small first printing, would be valuable; a first edition of his *The Old Man and the Sea*, which was published in huge numbers, is of far lesser value.

A beautiful binding may be worth something in itself if it is by a recognized artist, but its true value will depend upon the importance and scarcity of the book it encloses.

The same criteria apply to autographed copies. If it were, say, J.D. Salinger's *The Catcher in the Rye*, it would be a treasure. If, on the other hand, it's Jacqueline Susann's *Valley of The Dolls*, forget it—she traversed the country, autographing thousands of copies.

The autograph not of the author but of its owner, if that owner is famous enough, can also make a book rare. For example, it is well known that Marilyn Monroe long wanted to play the role of Grusha in Dostoyevsky's *The Brothers Karamazov* (the part in the movie went to Maria Schell instead). If you had even a Modern Library edition of the novel with Marilyn Monroe's signature in it, it would be rare and very valuable.

If you do own what you think might be a rare book, don't just rush off to the nearest dealer. Telephone a dealer or two, ask if they have a copy for sale and what the price is. This step has two purposes. First, if they say, "We wouldn't handle anything like that. Why don't you try a second-hand store," you will know your book isn't rare and will spare yourself a trip to the book shop and possible embarrassment. You also will have some idea of the market value of the book if indeed it is rare. Don't expect to get that full value, though; the rare book dealer you sell it to will want to make a profit.

RECORD BOOK ENTRIES

All professional sports keep track of their own records, from the most home runs in a season, to the most hockey goals in a play-off series. But then there are those people who are determined to make a mark for themselves in an offbeat way. They may want to beat the world record for standing absolutely still or for knocking over dominoes in one of those spectacular chain reactions that far exceed the drama politicians talk about in reference to Southeast Asia or Latin America.

If you would like to hold the world record in some offbeat activity or peculiar pastime, the bible you need to consult is the *Guinness Book Of World Records*. Don't confuse the *Guinness* editors with the producers of television shows that purport to show the unbelievable things that actual people do. *The Guinness Book Of World Records* is both a serious and a responsible publication, even though some entries may be bizarre. Its editors regularly eliminate categories from consideration that they feel have become too dangerous; for instance, they recently eliminated the sword-swallowing category.

To get into the pantheon of world-record holders, you must have at least two impartial expert witnesses present at the event. Expert means just what it says, and impartial means someone aside from close friends and relatives. If you want to be taken seriously, you should also arrange for local newspaper, radio, or television coverage of your attempt to beat the record. There is no particular form to be filled out, but if you are serious about setting a world record, you would be well advised to write in advance of your attempt to Guinness Superlatives, Ltd., 2 Cecil Court, London Road, Enfield, Middlesex, England. The telephone number is 01-441-367-4567.

RESUME REASONING

Many people have been tempted at one time or another to beef up their resume just a touch in order to appear a little more experienced, a little more impressive than they actually are.

Don't do it.

While it is true that many employers don't take the time to follow through and check every detail on a resume, you still may get caught later on. It's also going to make you nervous if you are hired. You've got to be prepared to continue the lie, or back it up with a further one, if the subject of your fabrication should inadvertently pop up. And, all too often, the subject will arise when you least expect it. Don't put yourself in the position of having to be constantly on guard: it will affect your emotional well-being and very likely your work.

Consultants on hiring are increasingly emphasizing to their corporate clients that past experience is less important than it has been cracked up to be. The past success does not ensure future success; nor does past failure dictate future failure. So don't try to outguess your possible employer. Say what you have done, and no more.

RICE, REALLY

Forget about quick-cooking or preprocessed rice. Convenient it may be, but it has nothing like the texture or flavor of real rice. If your rice turns out sticky and mushy, then you are doing something wrong.

The most commonly available real rice is long grain Carolina rice. Although Carolina is a brand name in the United States, this strain of rice, originally developed in the American South at the close of the seventeenth century, is now grown around the world and has supplanted many other strains, even in the Orient, where rice was first cultivated in at least 2000 B.C. Two other important strains of rice require mention. One is Basmati (sometimes spelled Basmatti) rice, another long-grain strain regarded as the "gourmet" rice in India and a number of other Middle Eastern and Far Eastern countries. It is narrower than Carolina rice and does not expand as much in cooking. Then there is Arborio rice, wider and oval in shape, from the Po Valley of Italy. Many (although not all) Italian chefs feel that the classic risotto of northern Italy should never be made with anything but Arborio rice.

Since the dishes in which Basmati and Arborio rice are used often involve specialized cooking techniques, for which recipes are available in numerous ethnic cookbooks, let us concentrate here on plain long-grain rice to be served as a side dish or a "bed" on which to ladle a stew or creamed entree.

There are three variables involved in cooking rice: the amount of rice, the amount of water, and the amount of heat. It's those variables that get people into trouble.

Let's take a standard recipe for cooking rice. *Bring two cups of water to a boil. Add one cup of rice, stirring to separate the grains. Cover tightly, lower the heat, and simmer for 20 minutes.*

Problems abound. If you stir too long, so much water will evaporate that there won't be enough left to cook the rice for an additional 20 minutes, even at a simmer. Then, there's that word simmer. Simmering means cooking below the boiling point. At a higher heat, the rice will absorb the water too quickly. Thus, you'll need to check the rice after 15 minutes to make sure there is enough water remaining to ensure tenderness and prevent scorching. If it is necessary to add additional water, make sure it too is simmering—adding cold water will turn the rice to mush. How much water should you add? That depends upon how close to being done the rice is. More variables!

There is an easier way.

First, to ensure that your rice won't be sticky, wash it in cold water. Nutritionists may bridle at this instruction, insisting that washing the rice removes valuable nutrients. So be it. Throughout the Orient, where rice has been the main staple of the diet for at least two thousand years, cooks wash their rice. That's why the rice in Oriental restaurants is so fluffy.

Now bring a quart of water to a boil in a large pot, add a cup of rice, stirring briefly, cover and boil for 15 minutes. Test the rice to see if it is tender. Drain the rice and return it briefly to the pot to dry it further, shaking the pot over the burner for no more than a minute.

This is a very ancient method of cooking rice, based on a practical response to a simple fact: you can't turn a log or a charcoal fire down to a simmer.

If you're concerned about the lost nutrients, here's another approach. Use the usual two cups of water to one cup of rice. Boil for five minutes, covered. Then transfer the rice, with the remaining water, to a wide shallow ovenproof dish, cover tightly (using foil if necessary), and continue cooking in a very slow oven (200 degrees Fahrenheit) for another 25 minutes.

Rice, really.

RIGHT-OF-WAY ON THE WATER

If you are in a boat that is under sail, you always have the right of way over a motorboat of any kind. (Technically, that would include an ocean liner or an aircraft carrier, but, practically, they simply cannot maneuver quickly enough to avoid you, so you'd better be prepared to get out of the way.)

While it is true that the sailboat, whether it is 10 or 50 feet long, has the right-of-way, you should be aware that there are many people who rent powerboats for the weekend who have no experience or knowledge at all and believe that they are just driving a car on the water. The powerboat that continues to bear down on you when it ought to be changing course can only be dealt with as a menace. If it hits you, you can certainly sue and win, but the better part of valor is to recognize when you are dealing with an untutored macho idiot, and change course. Get out of the way, take down the name of the boat, and report it to the harbor authorities or the Coast Guard when you get back to port.

In the case of two sailboats, the one that is close-hauled (tacking with the sail drawn in over the boat) has the right-of-way. If two sailboats are both tacking, the boat on the port tack must change course to avoid the boat on the starboard tack. Port? Starboard? There is an old saying that helps here: you get a star on the board if you are right. If you are tacking with the wind coming from your right, as you face forward, you are on a starboard tack and you have the right of way over the boat that has the wind filling its sails from the left, or port side.

Remember, however, that if your sailboat has an outboard motor, and you turn it on, you automatically become responsible for getting out of the way of any sailboat.

ROACH WARS

There are many biologists who believe that roaches are the most successful life form ever spawned on this planet. They were here millions of years before we were, and there is evidence that they are singularly impervious to radiation—thus they may be here millions of years after we are. They can eat almost anything, and in terms of fecundity they make the rabbit look like a rank amateur.

But we'd rather not, with all due respect to their biological superiority, have them running around our kitchens.

A New York City apartment dweller onne asked the exterminator, at the conclusion of his monthly visit, "Does that really do any good?" An honest man, he replied, "Are you kidding, lady? Once a month?"

If you've got a real problem, it's going to take several days of effort and upheaval to bring it under control. Start by searching for major nests, zapping the roaches with an aerosol can. Then move all foodstuffs out of your kitchen. You can either remove all utensils, pots, china and glassware beforehand, or wash them all afterward. Then close off the kitchen and set off a spray bomb. Then put down boric acid, in cracks, behind appliances and in the corners of cabinets. Boric acid is one of the few things that roaches haven't adapted to. If you have kids or pets, however, be sure they can't get at the boric acid; it will make them sick too. Ideally, everyone in an apartment building should follow this procedure simultaneously, since the roaches are likely to move to someone else's unbombed kitchen until the air has cleared in yours, and then move back again.

If you have only a few roaches, just use a spray can. But every time you buy a new can, change brands. They vary slightly in their ingredients, and by changing brands, you can keep the ever-adaptable roach off balance.

ROSE PRUNING

    Your neighbor, for many years a leading light of the local garden club, prunes her hybrid tea roses and floribundas back to about a foot from the ground each spring, just as they are beginning to bud. She also has some grandifloras; those she prunes to a height of 15 to 18 inches. You, however, favoring a much less drastic approach to pruning, simply remove the winter-killed upper portions of the canes to an inch or two below the point where the canes appear to be live and green. You have, like your neighbor, removed any canes that appear diseased, and others that rub against one another, in order to assure proper air circulation once the rose bushes leaf out. Still, the result is that your pruned bushes are a good third higher than your neighbor's. Who's right here?
    The answer is: Both approaches are right, though each will produce a different kind of rose. The controversy stretches as far back as rose-growing itself, and authorities can be cited to support either method. Even the growing and care instructions from two different nuseries, for example, Jackson & Perkins Co. and Star Roses, will often be at odds

on this issue.

If you want a lot of roses blooming profusely on a fairly high bush, then you should prune lightly. If, on the other hand, you want your bushes to bear a few extra-large "exhibition" roses, the kind that win prizes at the garden club, then you will be correct in pruning back more drastically.

Whichever approach you take, there is a universally agreed on technique for making a pruning cut. Cut downward toward the inside of the bush at a 45-degree angle with your pruning shears. (Don't use grass clippers or kitchen scissors, which might result in a ragged edge). As in the illustration, the cut should be made about a quarter-inch above an outside bud eye, which is recognizable as a reddish swelling on the cane.

Pruning, whether high or low, should be done in the early spring when the leaf-eye swellings first appear. If you wait until the new growth is more than two inches long, you're likely to cause damage.

RUNNING AT YOUR OWN SPEED

Many physicians and psychologists have begun issuing serious warnings about the physical and emotional dangers of becoming too caught up in the running and jogging craze that has swept the country. Even well-known runners and officials of running clubs have joined in saying, "Watch it," to the amateur runner. And the recent death of running guru James Fixx, who suffered a fatal heart attack while running, has given many people pause.

This isn't just a matter of proper equipment (see Jogging Shoes) but of physical and emotional health. Muscle and bone damage can result from trying to do too much too soon, and there is a serious possibility of a heart attack or stroke if you extend yourself beyond your natural limits. Physicians advise that anyone who is going to take up running, especially if that person has led a relatively sedentary life, should have a thorough physical first. If you are already a runner, or jogger, don't be influenced by the number of miles a friend says he or she runs a day. Even if the friend is your own age, he or she may be constitutionally fit to run much longer and much farther than you. Remember that we're all made differently: even among great runners, some find themselves superbly suited to short sprints but wouldn't dream of entering a marathon. Know your limits and stay within them.

Psychologists express concern, too, at the increasing numbers of addictive runners, people for whom running becomes an escape from reality. One California study found that a startlingly high level of marital discord and divorce existed among couples in which one partner was spending more than an hour a day running. The question to ask yourself is: are you running for your health, or are you running away from problems you don't want to face in your relationship?

SALT ON ICE

There's been a winter storm. On the radio the next morning it's announced that the Sanitation Department has been on the job all night, plowing and spreading salt. Main thoroughfares are clear. But there's still your front steps or front walk to take care of. The snow turned to rain at one point, and then the temperature dropped below freezing again. Your steps and walk are like glass, and somebody could have a bad fall. So you do what the professionals do—haul out the bag of salt you bought on special at the supermarket and start spreading the stuff around.

Before you do that, however, you should realize that a few bags of $1.98 salt can end up costing you hundreds of dollars in repairs to your property. Salt eats cement. It eats brick. It even eats concrete, asphalt, and tar, and almost anything else your front walk is composed of. It also destroys the roots of your grass, box hedge, or pachysandra. City sanitation departments use salt because it clears streets quickly; but take a look at the average city street and ask yourself if you want your own property to end up like that.

You're much better off using sand. It won't work as fast, and the steps may still be a little slippery. But it's the best bet in the long run.

SAND TRAPS

Your golf ball is in scruffy grass near the bottom of a three-foot wall on the side of the sand trap nearest the putting green. It's going to be a very tough shot to get the ball up over the lip of the trap and onto the green.

What club should you use?

Well, before you think too much about that, many professional golfers suggest you turn around and look behind you. Maybe the best way out of this predicament isn't to shoot toward the green, but backward onto the short grass of the fairway. From there, you have a clear shot over the trap, and with a little control, you might be able to put your ball very close to the pin. Backpedaling can sometimes be the smartest thing you can do.

SEASONING AND CLEANING A CAST-IRON SKILLET

A cast-iron skillet is one of the most "old-fashioned" cooking pots we have in this age of aluminum and Teflon. While it is not a good cooking medium for delicate sauces or poaching, it remains unsurpassed for many dishes. It conducts and spreads heat more evenly than any other kind of pot, and it can be heated to very high temperatures without damage. The renowned Creole chef Paul Prudhomme makes extensive use of cast-iron skillets—his celebrated Blackened Redfish could not be made without it.

A new cast-iron skillet must be seasoned before use. The skillet should be wiped on the interior, both sides and bottom, with vegetable oil (but don't use olive oil, which has too strong a flavor) and then set over moderate heat for 15 to 20 minutes. Once a cast-iron skillet has been seasoned, you should avoid washing it if possible. Instead, scour the interior with coarse salt. If you do wash it, use hot soapy water *immediately* after use, rinse, and set it over a low flame for a few minutes to dry out. If the pan is not thoroughly dried, rust can develop, requiring additional cleaning and reseasoning.

This may sound like a lot of trouble, but for the best hash-browned potatoes or fried fish you ever ate, a cast-iron skillet is the ticket.

SECOND OPINIONS

Second medical opinions can create problems for a variety of reasons. Some physicians pack you off for a second opinion at a moment's notice simply because they haven't the vaguest idea what's wrong with you—a growing problem in this age of specialization. When a major operation is involved, they may also want to protect themselves from a malpractice suit by soliciting the diagnosis of another expert. (Some people take the entirely reasonable attitude that if a doctor can't figure out what your problem is, he or she shouldn't charge you. But it doesn't work that way.)

The greater problem arises with doctors who feel their patients are betraying them by asking for a second opinion. They take it personally, right in the middle of their egos. Watchdogs of the medical profession, including a healthy number of responsible physicians, suggest that if your doctor discourages you from seeking a second opinion, or takes umbrage at the very idea, it's a very good reason to insist upon having one or to switch doctors altogether. But there is one thing you should never do: sneak off and get a second opinion without telling the original physician. That will only cause trouble all around, angering the doctor who made the first diagnosis, and putting the second doctor in a very awkward position.

You have every right to a second opinion (indeed, many insurance policies now cover an additional examination), and it may be extremely wise to seek one out. But be up front about it.

SEEDLINGS

The seed packet instructs you to thin the seedlings, whether you've planted them indoors or sown them directly in the garden in warmer weather, as soon as they reach a certain height—generally from one to three inches. Many people ignore this advice because they simply can't bear to pull out a "plant" that has sprouted. But you'd better do it. If you don't, even the larger, stronger seedlings are going to suffer, their roots crowding one another and unable to draw sufficient nutrients from the soil.

If you want healthy plants, you've got to thin the seedlings—and you've got to be ruthless about it.

SHAVING TIPS

It doesn't matter what kind of razor blade you use. It doesn't matter what kind of shaving cream or gel you use. If you want a clean comfortable shave, your face has got to be wet, the stubble soft and pliable, the pores open. If you shave as soon as you get out of the shower, your face will be ready for a good shave. But if you are giving yourself a second shave of the day, or don't have time to shower, leave the shaving cream on your face for at least two minutes before applying the razor. Otherwise you will inevitably encounter a painful pulling sensation and end up with an uneven and unsightly result. You have to give the cream time to do its softening work. Otherwise, for a quickie shave, you're better off with an electric shaver.

SKI WAXING

The television commentators at World Cup skiing competitions or the Olympics often emphasize the importance of ski waxing as a way of maximizing speed on variable snow and race-course conditions. In a race in which the top finishers may be separated by a mere hundredth of a second, there is reason to focus on such detail. But how much importance should the recreational skier give to ski waxing? Many ski instructors and top competitors feel that a lot of people get carried away with the waxing mystique and fail to understand the purpose of waxing.

First, you have to consider what kind of skiing you are doing and whether you're skiing to relax or to race. In Nordic (cross-country) skiing, which involves skiing up as well as down an incline, the wax is crucial: the right wax will give your skis grip uphill and permit you to glide smoothly downhill. With the wrong wax, you'll either slip or stick. Cross-country skiers select the right wax on the basis of the water content of the snow, consulting a chart (available at ski outfitters) that matches snow temperature and conditions to the color code of the appropriate wax.

In Alpine skiing, the object is to increase the speed, especially in downhill races; for the tight turns of the slalom and giant slalom, a combination of speed and grip is required. Thus a racer may use one wax on the tip of the ski and another on the tail. But the ordinary recreational downhill skier, more interested in safety and control than maximum speed, may not ever feel the need to wax his or her skis.

The fine points of ski waxing can only be learned through years of experience. Each individual skier gets to know how his or her skis perform in various conditions and learns to change the wax accordingly. Ultimately, waxing right is a matter of personal style and technique.

SKIDDING

The heavy rain has stopped, the sun has come out, and traffic is picking up speed, even though there are still stretches of wet pavement. Suddenly, your car begins to skid. Instinctively, you slam on the brakes and turn the steering wheel in the opposite direction of the skid. Unfortunately, this is one case in which your instincts are dead wrong.

The correct procedure is emphasized in driving manuals and driver-training courses; questions pertaining to skidding appear on written driver's license tests in numerous states. Nevertheless, according to the National Safety Board, improper reactions to skids remain a major cause of accidents. Part of the problem is that while people can be *told* what they ought to do, it's not something that can be practiced beforehand. And when it does happen, the wrong physical response often takes place before the driver has time to *think* about what he's supposed to do.

So drum it into your mind: what you need to accomplish is to get the wheels rolling again instead of sliding sideways. Immediately take your foot off the gas pedal, and steer in the direction of the skid. That may *feel* wrong, but it's what the laws of physics demand. The brake should be pumped *lightly* up and down; avoid pushing the brake all the way to the floor, as that will only decrease your control. Once you feel the wheels rolling forward again, you can begin, slowly, to steer in the opposite direction and, very lightly, apply your foot to the gas pedal.

SMOKE DETECTOR SENSE

Smoke detectors can save lives, and they are increasingly required by law in commercial buildings and rental apartments. But fire officials too often find in residential fires that the smoke detector has been disconnected. The reason is often that it kept going off at the slightest provocation, and the apartment or house occupants got sick of listening to the ear-piercing signal.

The problem, of course, is that the smoke detector was put in the wrong place to begin with. Don't install your smoke detector in a hallway right outside your kitchen; it will be going off constantly. Don't put it in a family room if there are heavy cigarette smokers in your family; again, you'll be plagued with false alarms. Exactly where a smoke detector belongs depends upon the layout of the particular abode, but generally speaking, it should be far enough from an exit so that the exit itself remains passable after the alarm goes off but away from areas where there is a normal concentration of heat or smoke. If it is too close to the exit, the smoke may be already dense once the alarm is triggered.

SPAYING OVERNIGHTS

You're having your female dog spayed. This operation to remove the ovaries and the uterine horns prevents the dog from going into heat and precludes pregnancy. Since it is an operation, you should not be surprised when the veterinarian tells you your dog will have to be kept at the clinic overnight or perhaps for two nights. But is this really necessary?

No responsible veterinarian is going to let you take your dog home the same day as the spaying unless he or she is confident that there will be no problems. If you're told that you must wait until the next day, accept the fact. But sometimes vets suggest an overnight stay because they want to spare the sensibilities of the dog owner. Your vet knows that the dog would be happier at home than in a cage, but he or she is reluctant to release her because of the number of people who have complained in the past about the shocking condition their beloved pet was in immediately after a spaying.

If you really want to have your dog the same day she is spayed, you should be prepared to find her in an extremely woozy state. The anesthetic will not have entirely worn off, and the dog even may have trouble walking and very likely will have to be carried up and down stairs. (Great Danes and other very large breeds obviously pose a problem.) In addition, and far more upsetting to most people, the dog's abdomen will be covered with dried blood all around the stitches

Thus many vets prefer to have the owners leave their dogs overnight. The next day the anesthetic has worn off, the dog is walking normally, and she has licked away all the dried blood. The dog owners feel a lot better about the operation, and the vet gets less grief.

If you still insist on having your pet back the same day, it's best to make it clear to the vet that you understand what shape she is going to be in. If you assure your vet that you can deal with the situation, he or she is much more likely to grant your request. You'll have your pet home sooner, and you'll also save yourself some money.

SPEED-READING

Have you ever bought a paperback novel, gotten 20 pages into it and then realized that you'd read the book before? You're probably a natural skimmer, or speed-reader. Skimming is fine if you just want to get the gist of something. And a speed-reading course can help slow readers to pick up the pace. But if you want to remember specific facts for more than a day, or to savor the language, you will have to actually read the book, not skim it.

Speed-reading is useful for getting acquainted with material that's not especially important in the first place. It's not for real learning or real enjoyment.

SPRAIN TREATMENT

The worst thing you can do after suffering a sprain is to apply heat, whether in the form of a hot water bottle, or worse, a commercial liniment designed to soothe aching muscles.

Heat will bring the blood to the surface and thus increase the swelling around the sprain, slowing the healing process, and even contributing to the pain. What you want is ice water—best for a sprained ankle is a bucket of water filled with ice.

Because a sprain can give you problems for six months or more, with damage to the ligaments, you have to be even more careful in treating it than a break. After the ice-water treatment, get the sprain X-rayed to make sure there is no break. If there isn't, you are in for a regimen of home treatment. Three or more times a day, plunge the sprained ankle into ice water, as cold as you can get it, and keep the foot there as long as you can stand it. Keep the foot elevated as much as you can the rest of the time—propping it up on a chair, putting a pillow under it while sleeping—and do as little walking as possible. When you do walk, put an Ace bandage on to provide support, and use a cane or even crutches, depending on the severity of the sprain.

Once the swelling has gone down, a new procedure starts. Continue to soak the foot in ice water, but then quickly plunge it into very hot water for a few minutes, to increase circulation. After that, put the foot right back into ice water to counteract any swelling. Repeat this procedure at least three times a day.

For a dancer or athlete, of course, there will also be exercises, as soon as the pain subsides enough, in order to get the strength back into the limb as quickly as possible. Even a nondancer should try holding the foot above the floor and rotating the ankle for several minutes at a time to restore flexibility.

This approach also works for a sprained wrist or knee, although if the problem is with the knee, ice packs, alternated with heating pads, are easier to deal with for obvious anatomical reasons.

STOPPED-UP SINKS

The dishes are washed. Or you've just finished shaving. You look down and the water is just sitting there in the sink, dank and filthy. You reach down into the depths, hoping that it's something still in the sink that you can pull out with your hand. No luck. Half an hour later the water is down to about an inch. So you pull out that can or jar of commercial drain opener, and read the instructions once again. You know the stuff is dangerous, it's got lye in it. Following the instructions, you sprinkle the crystals or pour in the liquid. That ought to do it. But ten days later you've got the same problem. And worse yet, you're making the plumber's job harder when you finally do call him or her in. The plumber can get scalded by the lye when he or she starts to take the pipes underneath the sink apart. The residual fumes alone can be harmful.

What's the right way? The right way is to have on hand a "plumber's helper," one of those rubber suction cups on a long stick. They're cheap and they last for years, and they do a better job of unplugging a stopped-up drain than anything you can pour down it. The trouble is that most people don't use them properly.

It's pointless to use them when the sink is full of water, you'll just splash the standing water all over yourself and the surrounding area. Get a pot and ladle out most of the water. Leave about an inch in the sink. Then start *working*. Most people who use the plumber's helper pump it up and down over the drain for two or three minutes and stop. Keep going. spend 10 to 15 minutes pumping up and down with the suction cup. Don't stop after five minutes just because the water has run out. The clog is lurking just a little farther down now. Run another inch of water into the sink and keep at it.

After 10 minutes, turn on the water full blast and watch how quickly it flows down into the drain. If it's *still* slow, go at it for another five minutes. And if you still haven't fixed it, then call the plumber. You've obviously got a major problem.

SUICIDE PREVENTION

Few human beings go through the stresses of a lifetime without contemplating suicide, if only fleetingly. Most of us quickly repress such thoughts and are shocked when someone we know or know of does commit suicide. Yet the fact remains that there are more suicides than homicides each year—it is a major mental health problem.

Suicide is an act of extremely complex dimensions, moral, religious, social, and psychological. Even the experts admit that the warning signals indicating a potential suicide are vague at best. Such indicators as loss of appetite, moodiness, irritability, and withdrawal may also be attributable to a wide variety of other problems. Many people who commit suicide appear to have been happy and productive right to the moment of taking their own lives. Suicide prevention is thus a difficult and mysterious business.

But there is one thing on which all the experts agree. *Never take a suicide threat lightly.* Even a passive threat, such as the remark, "I wish I could go to sleep and just never wake up," should be a cause for alarm and for action. Don't pass it off with mild solace. Start asking questions, trying to get the person who has confessed despair to discuss what he or she is feeling. Insist that the person seek counseling or at the very least that he or she talk about the problems with a family clergyman or physician. If the person balks at seeking help or backtracks and says, "Oh, I'm not really serious," don't just wash your hands of the matter. Call your local office of the Suicide Prevention League or a suicide hotline, and ask for advice. Take action.

SUNBURN SOLACE

It's the first summer weekend you've been able to get away, and you overdo it, spending too many hours in the sun. You've got a bad sunburn. Your shoulders and the backs of your legs and your thighs are the color of a cooked lobster. And that's just what you've done—cooked yourself.

You probably have only a first-degree burn, which affects the outer layer of the skin, but it's painful nevertheless. And because you've burned yourself over so much of your body, you may also be suffering from dehydration and fever. Physicians warn that many people take sunburn much too lightly. They strongly advise against using a lotion or spray that acts as a surface painkiller. That may reduce the pain, but as a result you may ignore other effects and resume strenuous activity. Don't.

Treat serious sunburn by applying wet cold compresses to all affected areas of the body, and stay away from the lotions until the pain begins to recede. Drink plenty of fluids to counteract dehydration, and take it easy physically. It's not just your skin that hurts; your entire system has received a shock. If there is any sign of blistering, you've got a second-degree burn and should see a doctor immediately to ensure that infection doesn't set in.

A sunburn is a burn. Treat it as such.

TASTEFUL COLOR COMBINATIONS

Once upon a time, in the late 1950s into the early 1960s, it was the height of fashion for men to wear pink shirts and black ties. That style went out of fashion with a vengeance.

And then there was the rule about *never* wearing brown shoes with a dark blue skirt or pair of trousers. Black was de rigeur with dark blue. The combination of blue and green has at various times been disdained as bad taste and lauded as the height of "sportiness." Not too long ago, such a color combination as mauve and orange would have been regarded as absolutely frightful. Yet in the 1980s, designers such as Rosita and Ottavio Missoni have become all the rage by combining colors that used to be regarded as "clashing."

The point is that we're dealing with taste, and taste changes constantly. Some colors do vibrate against one another, while others meld. Some combinations are startling, others soothing. It all depends on how they are used: what effect do you want? There will always be some arbiter of taste to declare that certain combinations are "tacky," and there will always be some designer a few years later who will make a fortune by defying such dicta.

If other people find your taste in color combinations peculiar, just remember that you are either ahead of or behind the times, avant-garde or retro. At some point along the way, every conceivable color combination will be or has been "in good taste." If you want to play it safe, though, stick to black and white, the only combination that has attained the status of classicism.

TICK REMOVAL

Ticks love dogs, and dogs love to roam where they are likely to pick them up. While flea/tick collars provide some protection, you should still inspect your dog for ticks, especially the hindquarters and inside the ears. Veterinarians recommend removing ticks by hand, grasping the tick as close to the skin as possible and pulling firmly without twisting. Many people find this an unpleasant task, particularly when removing a swollen female tick (male ticks do not swell). If you can't bear to touch the tick, use tweezers, but do not ever use the popular trick of applying a lighted match to a tick. Not only do you run the risk of singeing the dog's coat, but you may increase the chances of infection. It is also wrong to apply petroleum products to a tick, since the dog may subsequently lick the affected area.

Don't worry if the head of the tick remains in the dog's skin. The tick will not grow back, as superstition has it, nor does the remaining head necessarily cause infection. The area of the bite will become red and somewhat thickened, but that is a reaction to a chemical present in the tick's saliva. The spot should clear up in about two weeks.

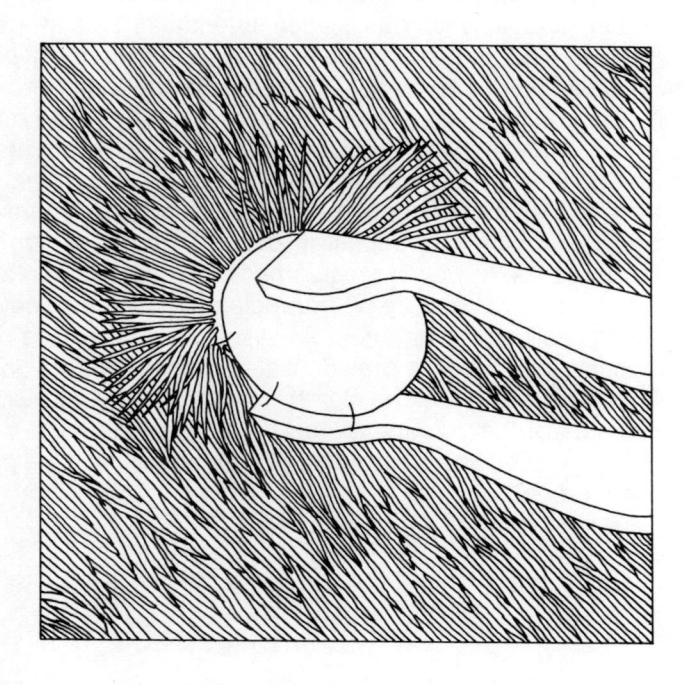

TIPPING ABROAD

American tipping practices very often do not apply in other countries. If you fail to acquaint yourself with the proper tipping procedure followed in the country, you could end up tipping double, failing to tip someone who expects it, or even causing trouble for someone who is legally or ideologically forbidden to accept a tip.

For example, in many foreign countries, restaurant or hotel service tips are included in the bill. But that practice can vary even within a single country. In France, where the practice is widespread, the bill should be marked *service compris* if service is included. This custom is particularly prevalent in expensive establishments; it may not be the case in a small bistro or out-of-the-way country hostelry. If you have *any* doubts, do as the French themselves do—ask. Even if the service is included, it is customary to leave a little extra change in a haute-cuisine restaurant or in any restaurant in which you are particularly pleased with the service. The same approach applies in most European countries, but not in England, where service is not included.

In many countries you are expected to tip people who do not customarily receive tips here; the list ranges from theater ushers in France, Spain, and Italy to gas station attendants who perform a service like checking your oil in Spain to flower sellers in Egypt. The amounts involved are usually small. Numerous guidebooks and travel books will give you specifics, including the proper sum to be offered.

There are also places where tipping is frowned on for a variety of reasons. In Japan it is a breach of etiquette in most situations. In the Soviet Union and China, accepting tips is a punishable offense (it's considered a symptom of capitalist decadence). In both these Communist countries, however, small American souvenirs, trinkets, or a pack of cigarettes will usually be appreciated. Just stay away from anything with political overtones. A Disneyland pin, yes (even Krushchev has been there); a presidential campaign button, no.

It's part of being a good traveler to familiarize yourself with the tipping practices of the country you are visiting. You'll make a good impression, and you'll come away with a good impression of the people who have served you.

TOY SAFETY

Despite the efforts of the Consumer Product Safety Commission and other agencies, the number of injuries that children suffer because of toys remains high. Surveys differ, but at least 125,000 such injuries are *reported* every year, many of them serious and some resulting in death. The greatest number of such incidents are caused by toys with sharp edges and by toys or broken pieces of toys that are swallowed.

But anyone buying a toy for a child should be concerned with more than the obviously dangerous. Many injuries could be avoided if greater attention were paid to the age of the child to whom a toy is being given. A toy that is well made and perfectly suitable to a six-year-old may result in an injury to a three-year-old. The current emphasis on teaching very young children to read and do mathematics—controversial in itself—has also led to giving young children "challenging" toys that are manufactured with an older age group in mind. The Consumer Product Safety Commission warns strongly against this practice. Always check the age labels on toy packages, and match it to the child. If you are uncertain, buy something else. The right toy for one child can be the wrong toy for a younger one.

TRAFFIC TICKET TALES

Traffic tickets are seldom undeserved, although almost everyone likes to pretend that they are outraged by the latest one *they* got. The highways and byways would be a lot safer if many more traffic tickets were passed out. Think about how many times you have said to yourself, as some car cuts in front of you at 70 miles an hour, "Why isn't there a cop around to nab that maniac?"

Still, excuses or good acting jobs do work occasionally. Women have traditionally had better luck in this game than men, although that may change somewhat as the number of policewomen increases. No policewoman is likely to fall for another woman bursting into tears of self-pity. One woman of the author's acquaintance, who has successfully employed this technique, advises that even if you do get a ticket anyway, you should never abandon your role and turn angry. It could make the cop angry enough to increase a discretionary fine. Just drive away crying. Others have had success feigning ignorance of English and chattering excitedly in a foreign language. French seems to work best, Spanish frequently backfires.

People do occasionally exceed the speed limit because of a genuine emergency, and in such cases police officers can be understanding. Under no circumstances, however, invent an emergency. The cop may offer to escort you to your destination, which could lead to serious repercussions.

No matter what, do not start telling the cop off. Think of him or her as a baseball umpire, and remember what happens to players or managers who become unduly exercised.

Of course, you could also drive within the legal speed limit.

TRUTH IN AGING

"At her death," the obituary reads, "the legendary actress was variously reported to be anywhere from 67 to 75 years old." When we read such a report, most of us automatically tend to believe the higher age, and with good reason. Millions of ordinary citizens, from housewives to business executives, subtract a few years from their actual age. And it seems like a perfectly harmless kind of deception.

But, depending on how you go about it, lying about your age can in fact cause you a lot of trouble in llter years. It's one thing if you just do it in conversation, but a lot of people get carried away with their own myth of youthfulness, and start lopping off a few years on official papers: insurance policies, employment applications, and the like.

When the time of life comes when you want to collect the *benefits* of your age in the form of Social Security Insurance, for example, you may have a problem. Unlike the general public, the Social Security Administration does not simply assume that the higher age is the truth. Proof is required. A birth certificate will be accepted as proof, but even if you have one on hand, a considerable delay can be involved before the bureaucracy will accept your plea that you've been subtracting from your actual age for 25 years. You could wait several months before the problem gets straightened out.

If you don't have a birth certificate, or have lost it, then you have got real trouble. In many areas of the country, birth certificates weren't issued until after the passage of the original Social Security Act in 1935. A child's name was entered in the family Bible, and that was it. Naturalized citizens who emigrated from strife-torn countries may find it impossible to produce any evidence of the date of their birth. And even if you are sure that your birth was officially recorded and the paper was filed in the county courthouse, you may discover that the building has burned down—or simply that you were "misfiled."

If you don't have a birth certificate—and millions of Americans do not—set about finding one if you've been lying about your age. And no matter how much you want to be thought of as young, never put anything but your correct age on any official piece of paper.

UMBRELLA OPENINGS

Statistics show that street crime decreases in bad weather. Even dedicated muggers would rather be inside, apparently, than brave the adverse elements (it's also more difficult, of course, to make a fast getaway on a rain-slicked or snowy sidewalk). On the other hand, perfectly law-abiding citizens arm themselves on rainy days with a dangerous weapon: the spring-operated automatic umbrella. Given the way many people go about opening these contraptions, a license ought to be required for carrying one.

There are several unsafe methods of opening automatic umbrellas—to one side, directly in front of you, or, most dangerous of all, at eye level. You can easily knock another pedestrian off his or her feet or strike someone in the face with a spoke using any of these methods. The problem is that other people, carrying already opened umbrellas, may not be aware of the menace until it is too late. They are looking at the sidewalk, trying to avoid puddles, or have their umbrellas pulled down closely over their heads, blocking their peripheral vision.

There is only one right, safe way to open an automatic umbrella. You have to hold it as high over your head as possible, press the button, and release the spring. You may get a few more raindrops on you, but you won't put out anyone's eye. And if you are a short person, you should take extra precautions. High over *your* head may be at someone else's eye level. Look before you press.

UNION JOINING

There are basically two kinds of unions. There are long-established unions that make it difficult for you to join because their interest lies in seeing that their present members are fully employed. The building trades are a classic example. And then there are unions that are still trying to build membership and a power base or are attempting to unionize a particular occupation or area of the country where they have run into strong opposition. Teachers, especially those at the college level, are a target of recruitment, as are textile and agricultural workers in the South and West.

If you want to join a union, the best way to learn the ropes is through a relative or friend who is lready a member. The bureaucracy of many unions is almost impenetrable unless you have a personal guide or "sponsor." This is one case in which the individual connection is essential. The "old-boy" network is not just a reality of Ivy League colleges and state universities; it is also very much in effect at the blue-collar level in terms of union joining.

Here are some questions to ask of someone who is already a member of a union you are thinking of joining:

1. How much, in dollar amounts or percentage of your paycheck will you have to pay in union dues?
2. What kinds of protection does your union offer in terms f working conditions?
3. Has the person ever been involved in a strike and how did it affect him?
4. What strike benefits are offered?
5. What benefits, if any, are available if you are laid off?

In some cases, you may want to ask yourself whether it is really to your advantage to join a union—at least just yet. Actor's Equity is a case in point. The members of Actor's Equity are 95 percent unemployed. Despite the fact that there are a great many non-Equity theaters around the country, many actors feel they haven't arrived, aren't true "professionals" unless they belong to the union. Many a young performer, after working steadily for two or three years in non-Equity summer stock or dinner theaters, finally manages to realize the dream of becoming a union member—and then doesn't work for a year or more.

If you can't work without joining a union, you have no choice. But if you can work, and are working, you may want to think twice about subjecting yourself to the rules and regulations that can, unhappily, make it *more* difficult to get other jobs.

V.D. AWARENESS

The sexual revolution, according to many commentators and surveys, has come and gone. There is evidence that it was to some extent specious in the first place, that it merely gave people the freedom to boast about what was once a dirty secret. But it has left us a disturbing legacy.

Veneral disease, once thought to have been brought under control, is rampant. Gonorrhea bacteria have mutated, becoming resistant to the drugs previously used to combat them. Syphilis, too, shows signs of resurgence. Genital herpes has made all the magazine covers. And then there is AIDS, most frightening to many because it is lethal, although there is increasing evidence that this is not a new disease, but rather one that has only recently been recognized as a distinctive problem (it apparently has existed in Central Africa for centuries).

Putting aside the question of promiscuity, the spread of veneral disease is fostered by ignorance of the signs of infection, and by an unwillingness to seek medical advice because of shame or fear. Any unusual physical manifestation in the genital area, including discharge, sores, swollen glands, persistent itching, or pain should be cause enough to see a physician. The problem may not be related to veneral disease, but it should be investigated. Such signs are often external in a man and thus easier for both the man and a partner to recognize. Among women, the indications are more likely to be internal, making them more difficult to detect.

Many people are particularly concerned about herpes. Herpes is a viral infection that takes two forms. Type one results in the common cold sore that appears on the mouth during an upper respiratory infection. It is type two that causes a veneral outbreak. The relationship between the two types is still being investigated, and while promising antidotes and possible cures are being tested, it may be years before they are approved for marketing. In the meantime, treatment involves reducing inflammation and pain.

In the case of AIDS, a "cure" appears to be even further in the future, although a suspicious virus called HTLV-3 has been isolated. AIDS victims to date have been almost entirely homosexual men, intravenous drug users, and, because of infected blood supplies, hemophiliacs.

How can V.D. be avoided? Physicians say that the use of a condom can offer some protection, and that thorough washing of the genitals with hot water and soap both before and after having sex may help, but that the only certain way to be safe is to limit oneself to a single, uninfected partner.

WAITER, WAITER

In a restaurant or cafe with first-rate service, there should never be a problem about attracting the attention of a waiter or waitress. A good waiter or waitress will regularly cast a quick glance in the direction of any table he or she is serving. Unfortunately, many restaurants are understaffed, and a lot of waiters seem to be equipped with built-in blinders. According to the arbiters of etiquette, the correct way to attract a waiter's attention in the United States, is to raise a hand above one's head and motion the waiter to your table. Some people have mastered the art of doing this with authority, but many of us carry it off with all the panache of a fourth-grader asking permission to go to the bathroom. Don't turn your hand palm outward and flap it about; that is gauche. Instead, hold your upraised hand, palm inward, with the index and middle finger raised, and the last two fingers bent inward over the palm. If it is the check you want, once you have attracted the waiter's attention turn your hand over and make a writing gesture in the air. This is a gesture understood all over the world.

If you actually have to call out, "Waiter," or "Waitress," it means that the service is not up to snuff. Waiters often take this as a reprimand (which, in essence, it is), so speak firmly but not sharply, or your service may get even worse. It helps to smile, a sign of forgiveness, when the waiter responds to your call.

Many foreign countries have more efficacious rules when it comes to getting a waiter's attention. In Spain, for instance, it is permissible in many situations to clap one's hands together twice in rapid succession. Don't try clapping your hands in Italy, however; it will be taken as an insult. The accepted practice in Italy is to rap a spoon lightly against a glass or coffee cup. Unhappily, these customs are becoming less common with the great increase in tourism. In the dining room of an "international" hotel or an haute-cuisine restaurant, the raised hand has come to replace the more direct hand-clapping or glass-rapping. Observe your fellow diners, and do what others do. But do it with authority. You are paying, after all.

WART WORRIES

No, you don't get warts from frogs. Warts are caused by a virus that attacks tiny cuts. Are they contagious? The answer is yes and no. They are seldom passed directly from one person to another, but if you pick at a wart, the virus may attack other areas of your own body where the skin is broken.

Most warts do not need any special attention. In most cases they eventually burn themselves out and fall off. However, if they are particularly unsightly, or located in a place that causes discomfort, you may want to purchase an over-the-counter remedy such as Compound W that will hasten the process of "drying out" the wart.

Put aside your superstitions and any ideas that warts are a sign of "uncleanliness." They are just one more of the small annoyances that the flesh is heir to.

WHO'S ON FIRST?

You are taking—perhaps dragging—a friend, romantic interest, client, or child to a sporting event about which you know a great deal and your guest knows very little. You want that person to enjoy the sport as much as you do. You are also, most likely, going to be tempted to show off your expertise.

Don't.

It doesn't matter whether the sport is baseball, football, tennis, or even a figure-skating competition. Anybody who has ever had his or her ear bent about every move that's being made on the field, the courts, or the ice, knows how confusing this rush of information can be and how embarrassed one can feel at not developing an instant grasp of bunting strategy, a quarterback sneak, charging the net, or the fact that that spectacular triple jump on the ice wasn't really very good because the skater's leg wasn't properly extended on landing.

Skip the details. Answer questions when you're asked, but don't let your blood pressure rise if you're told, "Well, I still don't understand."

WINE STORAGE

If you have even a casual interest in fine wines, you will already know that wine bottles should be stored on their sides in order to keep the cork damp—if the bottle were stored upright, the cork could dry out, allowing air to enter and thus spoiling the wine. You may also be aware that, ideally, wine should be stored at a temperature of 55 degrees. This is often difficult to achieve without purchasing an expensive refrigerated wine closet. But so long as the temperature remains reasonably constant, or rises and falls only gradually, your wines will not suffer unduly. The higher the temperature, however, the more rapidly the wine will age in the bottle, and it may have to be drunk before it has reached its optimum age.

There is one aspect of wine storage, however, that many people have wrong notions about. This concerns the regular turning of the bottles in their racks or bins. Don't do it. The supposed "need" to turn wine bottles is a myth. Terry Robards, author of *The New York Times Book of Wine*, speculates that this myth arose from the process used in the making of champagne, which calls for the bottles to be turned and shaken in order to help settle any sediment at the cork end before the champagne is disgorged and recorked. No wine, or champagne for that matter, should be turned or shaken after it has reached the market. Indeed, the more quietly it rests, the more contentedly it will mature.

WINNING THE LOTTERY

Sociological studies indicate that those who invest most in lottery tickets are in the lower-income brackets. It's their only hope of getting rich. But even if you're well-off already, you may still be tempted to play, and naturally you'll want to win.

Those who have hit lottery jackpots usually have adopted one of these four major winning strategies.

1. Choose numbers with personal meaning. Birth dates, wedding anniversaries, etc. Many winners have chosen this method.
2. Stick to the same numbers week after week, year in and year out. A recent New York State winner of three million dollars bet exactly the same numbers for five years.
3. Choose different numbers every time, at random. Another recent winner of the New York State biweekly lottery had forgotten his glasses and couldn't see the numbers of the card on which you must black out six choices. He did it, literally, blindly.

If you find number three discouraging, here's the real kicker.

4. Bet once or twice a year. A number of major winners in several states almost never buy lottery tickets, but just happened to buy one on a lark that brought them a fortune.

There are also those who bet on the basis of dreams or consultation with a fortune teller, those who pray for guidance, and those who put numbers into a dish at home and simulate a random drawing.

Good luck! But if you do win, prepare yourself to get an unlisted telephone number. H. Roy Kaplan, a sociologist who published a book called *Lottery Winners* in 1978, reports that almost all major winners found themselves harassed to the point of nervous collapse by people who wanted a handout—not just long-lost relatives and friends, but total strangers from across the country and around the world. If you win the lottery, everyone will think you owe them a piece of your luck—in cash, please.

XENOPHOBIC PROTOCOL

Xenophobia is the unreasonable fear or hatred of strangers or foreigners. It is included here not merely because it is one of the few actual words beginning with X but because it is a condition from which many Americans suffer, to their own cost and the detriment of the country's reputation.

Social historians explain that World War II brought about a revolution in isolationist attitudes as millions of our boys in uniform were shipped overseas to fight on foreign soils around the globe. And indeed, Americans have become much more sophisticated about other societies and are traveling abroad in unprecedented numbers. But that does not mean that the "ugly American" has disappeared. The species remains very much alive and unrepentant. They want to see the foreign "sights," from the Eiffel Tower to the Taj Mahal, but they expect the food, service, and general amenities to conform with what they'd get back home.

Snails? Are they trying to poison me?

Tip the usher? Are they trying to rob me?

What do you mean the shower is down the hall? Disease!

For these people, the package tour was invented. They can travel the world, staying in American-owned hotels, eating steak and baked potatoes, speaking nothing but English, see all the sights and learn absolutely nothing.

See PACKAGE TOURS for ways to enjoy the convenience of tours but still actually *experience* the places you are visiting.

ZODIAC TALK

Polls indicate that about 30 percent of the population takes astrology very seriously, about 40 percent thinks it is utter nonsense, and the remaining 30 percent finds it interesting but places little or no faith in its dicta about personality or its predictions.

There are indications that those who subscribe to astrology completely and those who dismiss it out of hand may both be wrong. Many distinguished scientists anddresearchers at universities around the world have long been investigating one aspect of astrology that they believe can be taken very seriously: that natural forces at work in the universe beyond the earth *do* have an effect on physical, chemical, and biological phenomena that occur on the earth. Whether such effects are due to radiation, gravitational forces, or a combination of several known and unknown factors is far from certain, but scientists concur that there is good reason why human beings, as far back as the Sumerians and Chaldeans of 5,000 years ago, have been concerned with the effects of the planets and the stars upon our own world.

One of the most eloquent researchers in this field has been Michel Gauquelin, a French psychologist and statistician who is the author of *The Scientific Basis of Astrology*. Gauquelin thoroughly demolished most of the mumbo jumbo that surrounds astrology, stating that "To predict the future by consulting the stars is to delude the world, or at least to delude oneself." Yet, in collecting statistical data on more than 30,000 individuals over the course of many years in many different countries, he found—somewhat to his dismay—that the correlation between the position of the planets at the hour of birth and the eventual choice of profession by these individuals far exceeds the laws of chance. He does not pretend to understand why this should be so, but he believes strongly that exploring the possible reasons *why* it occurs is the province and the responsibility of scientists. Astrology, he feels, was "man's first attempt to conceptualize the world." Much of that conceptualization is mired in magic and superstition, which he and other researchers reject. But they cannot ignore the kernel of truth that remains when the hocus-pocus is stripped away.

Thus, perhaps the right way to approach astrology is with tolerant skepticism for its excesses, including its focus upon minute predictions concerning our daily lives, but with respect for the fact that there may indeed be "more things in heaven and earth" than are dreamt of in our philosophy.